Hudson Bay

QUEBEC

D

A

NEWFOUNDLAND

NEW BRUNSWICK

Saint John

Montreal

Ottawa

VER.

NEW HAMPSHIRE

MASS

Boston

CONN

RHODE ISLAND

WISCONSIN

MICHIGAN

NEW YORK

New York

NEW JERSEY

Atlantic Ocean

Grand Rapids

Milwaukee

PENNSYLVANIA

Pittsburgh

DELAWARE

Chicago

Toledo

OHIO

Washington DC

MARYLAND

Moines

A

Indianapolis

Cincinatti

WEST VIRGINIA

VIRGINIA

MISSOURI

Louisville

St. Louis

KENTUCKY

NORTH CAROLINA

TENNESSEE

Nashville

ARKANSAS

Memphis

SOUTH CAROLINA

Little Rock

ALABAMA

Atlanta

MISSISSIPI

Birmingham

GEORGIA

LOUISIANA

Jackson

Jacksonville

New Orleans

FLORIDA

Gulf of Mexico

Miami

Zone 1 below −50°	Zone 3 −35° to −20°	Zone 5 −10° to −5°
Zone 2 −50° to −35°	Zone 4 −20° to −10°	Zone 6 −5° to 5°

Zone 7 5° to 10°	Zone 9 20° to 30°
Zone 8 10° to 20°	Zone 10 30° to 40°

Azaleas

To my Mother
who taught me to love flowers

SERIES EDITOR · VINCENT PAGE

AZALEAS

Christopher Fairweather

Photographs by Vincent Page

The
Globe
Pequot
Press

Chester, Connecticut 06412

First American edition published in 1988 by
The Globe Pequot Press, Chester, Connecticut 06412.

Library of Congress Cataloging-in-Publication Data

Fairweather, Christopher.
Azaleas.

(Classic garden plants)
Includes index.
1. Azalea.   I. Title.   II. Series.
SB413.A9F35   1988   635.9′3362   88–4292
ISBN 0-87106-729-3

Produced by the Justin Knowles Publishing Group,
9 Colleton Crescent, Exeter, Devon, England

Design: Gilvrie Misstear
Photographs: Vincent Page
Illustrations: Vana Haggerty
Zone map courtesy Swallow Books Ltd

Manufactured in Portugal

CONTENTS

LIST OF PLATES

FOREWORD

I am delighted and honoured to have been asked to write this foreword to Christopher Fairweather's excellent and informative new book on azaleas. These plants have a fascinating history, as the author so lucidly explains, and their beauty should certainly grace the gardens of all of us who are fortunate enough to have lime-free soil. (For those of us not so lucky, this book describes how we may grow these plants in containers and still enjoy their lovely colours.)

Evergreen azaleas, at their best in massed groupings, display their gentle colours in many of the world's beautiful gardens, some of which are listed in an appendix to this book. The evergreens are at their most specialized in Japan, where their cultivation takes a uniquely stylized form. The subtler, generously flowered, deciduous azaleas are also rightly and universally popular for the bright colours they contribute to our gardens. The great secret of success in planting these shrubs is to give thought to blending their colours and to use whites to heighten or soften the overall effect.

I am glad to see the Exbury Gardens featured in the text and photographs in this book. My father, Lionel de Rothschild, created these gardens, carried on in them the hybridizing work on azaleas that had been started at Knap Hill, and eventually produced the Exbury strain of deciduous azaleas.

It is a pleasure for me, too, to remember that Christopher Fairweather began his horticultural career at Exbury. Now, in this comprehensive and practical book, he sets out with admirable clarity all the information we need to choose and grow the azaleas that will best enhance our gardens, be they large or small.

Edmund de Rothschild

INTRODUCTION

I started my horticultural training in the early 1950s at the world-famous Exbury Gardens in Hampshire in the south of England – over two hundred and fifty acres filled with rhododendrons and azaleas. Very soon I was fired with enthusiasm for these wonderful plants.

I well remember the first task I was given. I joined a small team that, under the eye of an expert propagator, was putting evergreen azalea cuttings into propagating boxes. In two months we dealt with about fifty thousand cuttings. It sounds repetitious and tedious, but I enjoyed every moment of those early days. We started at 7.30 a.m. with a trip into the garden to collect the day's supply of cuttings. It was high summer and it was important that we took the cuttings in the cool of morning and then kept them in the shade under the greenhouse bench. The cuttings were trimmed to about 2in (5cm) and their lower leaves removed; then they were dipped into rooting powder and put into the propagating boxes. The boxes, which stood in long, neat rows, were about 18in (45cm) long and 12in (30cm) wide and were filled with a mixture of peat and sharp sand. The cuttings were lightly watered in and the boxes covered with a sheet of glass and shaded with newspaper. It was while I was doing this work that I first encountered the unique, spicy smell characteristic of azalea cuttings.

During my first spring at Exbury we prepared specimen azaleas to make a display at the Chelsea Flower Show in London, Britain's most prestigious annual horticultural event. We lifted the plants with great care and wrapped the roots in fine chicken wire. The great skill in this operation was to ensure that the plants were in perfect condition for the show. The then head gardener was expert at this; he could judge almost to the hour when the azaleas would be in full flower. The lifted azaleas were at first kept in the cool shade of some dense evergreen oaks to check any premature flowering. A week or so before the show they were moved to a cool greenhouse. There they were fine-mist sprayed at regular intervals and shaded if the weather warmed up or given more heat if it turned colder. With such close attention to detail, these magnificent specimen azaleas, in some cases 3–4ft (90–120cm) across, arrived for the show in perfect condition, with the whole of the plant covered and coloured with flowers.

By then I had acquired an admiration for the azalea that I have never lost. Azaleas, whether evergreen or deciduous, are marvellous shrubs for the garden. Each spring they can be guaranteed to give a riot of colour, in shades ranging, in the evergreens, from white to pink, lavender, orange, red, and hot scarlet and, in the deciduous, from white again to cream, egg-yolk yellow, orange, pink, and brilliant red. Added to all this we have in many varieties a bonus of lovely autumn colour. The leaves of 'Palestrina' turn to gold and yellow in early autumn and those of 'Hino Crimson' and 'Mother's Day' are suffused with red-bronze all through the winter. Perhaps the most dramatic autumn colours can be found among the deciduous azaleas; the best performer is *Rhododendron luteum (Azalea pontica)*, which puts on a display of scarlet and gold almost as fantastic as that of the Japanese maples.

Other advantages that azaleas offer to the gardener add to my enthusiasm for them. Under the correct soil conditions they are surprisingly easy to grow and are resistant to many pests and diseases. Because they have a very fibrous root system they can be lifted and moved around the garden with minimum disturbance at nearly all stages of growth.

And then there is their perfume. To walk through a woodland garden crowded with azaleas in full flower, especially on a warm evening after spring rain, is a really wonderful experience. I still remember magic evenings at Exbury during the peak of the flowering season when the evening air was saturated with the delicate, sweet scent of deciduous azaleas.

Christopher Fairweather

A HISTORY OF AZALEAS

The name is derived from the Greek word *azaleos*, which means 'dry'. This, to say the least, is unhelpful – azaleas, in fact, have little tolerance of drought. But they will thrive in a fair degree of heat, and perhaps that gives some justification for the Greek description. If you turn to a modern dictionary it will tell you that an azalea is an ericaceous plant formerly held to be a separate genus but now considered as a group within the genus *Rhododendron*. So that is not much more helpful; it tells you only that an azalea has to be a rhododendron but that not every rhododendron is an azalea. It is possible to attempt other distinctions – for example, that unlike other deciduous rhododendrons deciduous azaleas do not have scaly leaves – but they are not particularly helpful.

Nevertheless, people like me who love azaleas generally know one when they see one. In time, one's eye comes to recognize some sort of family characteristic that identifies a particular rhododendron as an azalea. So, looking at it pragmatically, it makes sense in practical gardening terms to forget academic distinctions and to treat these beautiful plants as a group.

It was in Japan that azaleas first found their way into cultivation. After more than four centuries the descendants of those plants are still furnishing gardens in suitable soils and climates all over the world. These earliest cultivars were evergreen azaleas, which were able to interbreed and hybridize together. However, the first azaleas to appear in European gardens (apart from some plants of *R. indicum*, which reached Holland in the 17th century and were subsequently lost) were deciduous types. Whereas evergreen azaleas originate from only a relatively limited part of the globe, deciduous azaleas occur naturally on three continents, and those from Turkey, the Far East, and both coasts of the United States can, with varying degrees of success, be interbred like members of a continuous race. So the story of the development of the two types of azalea is really two stories, and it is simplest to deal with them separately.

Behind the wide range of rhododendrons which is available to gardeners today lies the great adventure story of the plant-hunting expeditions that, starting in the late 19th century and continuing even more intensively in the early 20th century, explored the mountain peaks and jungles of, especially, south-east Asia. The story of azaleas is an adventure too, but an intellectual rather than a physical one. The plants themselves were not so difficult to find because they were in relatively accessible parts of the world. The adventure came in the breeding and hybridization of the plants to give us the immense range and variety of brilliant azaleas that we can grow in our gardens today.

The Story of Deciduous Azaleas
Hybridization is the mating of two distinct species to produce an offspring that belongs to neither but combines certain qualities of each. Deliberate hybridization aims to combine the most desirable qualities of the two parent species, in a way that nature happens not yet to have accomplished – for example, to combine the hardiness of one parent with the large blooms of the other.

The first hybridizations were made in the early 19th century. The first recorded one of all was apparently an accidental crossing between *A. periclymenoides*, an American member of the sub-species *R. luteum*, and *R. ponticum*, the common mauve plant that has spread in many wild woodlands and become naturalized in some parts of Britain. The product of this unlikely cross was called an 'azaleadendron'. It is not the only example of a hybrid bridging between the azalea series and the rest of the rhododendron genus, but there is no other that is at all well known. The resulting plant, *R. hybridum*, was added to the collection of the Royal Botanic Garden in Edinburgh in 1814.

Some of the early records give us a few interesting clues to the first azalea arrivals into Britain. Philip Miller, who worked at the Chelsea Garden in London from 1722 to 1770, during this time wrote *The Gardeners' Dictionary*. The seventh edition, which came out in 1759, talks in general terms of both rhododendrons and azaleas (meaning deciduous azaleas). The eighth edition, of 1768, specifically names *R. russatum*, a mountain species from China, and *R. ferrugineum*, a common native of the European Alps and the Pyrenees which we know as the Alpine rose. What is interesting to us is that Philip Miller goes on to say that: 'there are other species of this genus which grew naturally in the Eastern countries, and others are natives of America, but the two sorts I have mentioned are all I have seen in the English garden.' Which is to say that he had not set eyes on any azaleas yet, although some had already reached Britain. In a later edition Miller mentions *R. calendulaceum (A. calandulacea)*, an American species which was introduced by seed perhaps as early as 1734. He says also that: 'other interesting azaleas grow in the Pontic area of Turkey, and others in India, but as neither of these are in English gardens I shall not elaborate on them.' Of course the first azalea mentioned by Miller, *R. luteum*, which was introduced in 1793, is as popular today as ever – sweet-scented, it has perhaps the most stunning autumn colour of any azalea (see page 50).

By the early 19th century there was much British interest in rhododendrons and azaleas as garden plants, and surprisingly high prices were being paid for them. We have records of a sale conducted by a Mr Pewick, at which 'a considerable number of azaleas formed the choicest part of the collection, and sold at high prices, one of them producing 20 guineas'. But it was in the middle of the century that the main introductions started to arrive. In 1848 and 1849 Sir Joseph Dalton Hooker collected and described more than forty new species of rhododendrons, and that amounted to more than the total number then in cultivation. He sent drawings and descriptions of them back to England, where they were published in his book *Rhododendrons of Sikkim-Himalaya*, which caused a great sensation. Only a minority of the rhododendrons described in it were members of the azalea series, but one of them, *R. molle*, is perhaps the most important discovery of all among the deciduous species.

Alongside the collectors, the hybridizers had also been at work. In the Belgian city of Ghent, between 1804 and 1834, a baker named P. Mortier began producing the Ghent hybrid azaleas. He used three American species of the azalea series – *R. calendulaceum*, *R. nudiflorum*, and *R. speciosum* – together with the scented *R. luteum* from around the Black Sea to produce some robust, sweetly scented, and hardy plants. Although most of the Ghent hybrids have now been superseded by more modern varieties, some are still available, including 'Gloria Mundi' and the tangerine-red 'Coccinea Speciosa', a beautiful June-flowering azalea (see page 41). All the Ghents that are still grown have great charm. Generally the flowers are plentiful though small, and many of them are double, such as the popular soft-yellow 'Narcissiflora' (see page 66). Not everyone cares for double flowers now, but they suited the taste of the late 19th century for fashion and finery. So, about the same time we find another group of deciduous azalea hybrids being produced, also in Belgium. These were the Rustica and Flore Pleno hybrids, which are all double flowered and which come into bloom a week or two later than the Ghents.

In Holland as well as Belgium there were important developments in hybridization. In Boskoop the nursery firm of M. Koster and Sons carried out some exciting work on deciduous azaleas around 1895. By crossing *R. occidentale* with Mollis azaleas they produced some marvellous fragrant flowers with delicate colours. A few of these are still in cultivation, including the lovely *A. delicatissima*, which is soft yellow in the bud and opens to cream, and the beautiful 'Exquisite' and 'Graciosa'.

The English contribution to the range of deciduous azalea hybrids has been very great. At the start, much of the work was centred upon the Knap Hill gardens near Bagshot in Surrey, where Anthony Waterer was involved in a breeding programme that produced many outstanding azaleas. Other superb hybrids were produced at Wisley, the home of the Royal Horticultural Society's gardens. Here the plants were given, rather oddly, the names of rivers – for example, 'Avon', 'Medway', 'Stour', 'Cam', 'Frome', 'Tay', 'Thames', and 'Trent'. The Knap Hill azaleas were for the most part named after birds – 'Bullfinch', 'Buzzard', 'Gannet', 'Golden Oriole', 'Kestrel', 'Lapwing', 'Penguin', 'Redshank', and 'Whitethroat'.

Another garden of great importance in the azalea story was Exbury in the New Forest, where, in the early years of this century, Lionel de Rothschild continued working with the Knap Hill azaleas and conducted an extensive and elaborate series of experiments in hybridization. To Exbury, perhaps more than any other garden, we owe a large number of the exciting plants we enjoy today. The Exbury/Knap Hill azaleas were more imaginatively named – they include 'Ballerina', 'Firefly', 'Hotspur', 'Gibraltar' (see page 74), 'Annabella', 'Tangier', 'Pink Delight', 'Soft Lips', and 'Bright Straw'. The plants that were used for breeding at Exbury came from various sources. Most perhaps came from Knap Hill, but some were home-bred at Exbury and later used as stock. Some of these Exbury stock plants are still grown widely today, including 'Strawberry Ice', 'Royal Lodge', 'Gallipoli' (see page 55), 'Golden Horn' (see page 38), 'George Reynolds', 'Cecile' (see page 56), 'Berryrose (see page 52), 'Basilisk', and 'Brazil'.

Some years afterwards a New Zealand grower, Edgard Stead, imported some Exbury stocks and developed an independent strain at his Ilam estate near Christchurch. He brought larger blooms, later flowering, and greater fragrance to the Exbury range. The orange-to-red Ilam azaleas, in particular, became commercially successful in the United States. The Ilam plants were further developed by another New Zealander, J. S. Yeates. From seeds sent from New Zealand an American breeder, David G. Leach, grew thousands of plants for the American market. Several of these – such as 'Canterbury', 'Maori', and 'Spring Salvo' – are now numbered among the most popular of the azaleas to be seen in American gardens.

The Story of Evergreen Azaleas

It would not be fair to say that the hybridization of deciduous azaleas has ground to a halt – except in Minnesota, where work goes on to develop the 'Northern Lights' azaleas. But it is certainly true that the emphasis is increasingly being thrown upon evergreen azaleas.

First of all, let us try to clear up some confusions and define our terms.

Evergreen azaleas are not truly 'evergreen' in quite the usual sense of the word. Their foliage is dimorphic, which means simply that they have two kinds of leaves. Spring leaves appear, distributed along the branches, at, or just after, flowering time. They fall in autumn, often turning yellow before they do so. Other leaves unfold in early summer; they are thicker, smaller, more leathery, and darker than the spring leaves and they are crowded at the tips of the branches.

They are usually shed in the following spring, although in some species, such as *R. indicum*, they may last for up to three years. These second leaves often turn reddish during the winter and, if the weather is really cold, most of them drop in any case.

Evergreen azaleas are often casually referred to as Japanese azaleas. This is misleading, because not all the original stock plants come from Japan nor have all the hybrids been produced in Japan. It is also muddling, because it gives rise to confusion over *R. japonicum*, which is a deciduous azalea, of the sub-series Luteum.

All the evergreen azaleas originate in Asia. All except *R. tashiroi* (which has its own sub-series, Tashiroi) belong to the sub-series Obtusum. According to the Royal Horticultural Society's Rhododendron Handbook, the sub-series contains forty species, of which twenty-four are not in cultivation. Of the remaining sixteen species, about half have been extensively used in hybridization, the main ones being *R. mucronatum*, *R. linearifolium*, *R. indicum*, *R. kaempferi* (see pages 52–3), and *R. kiusianum*.

It is in fact doubtful whether the first two of these, *R. mucronatum* and *R. linearifolium*, are true species; they have been cultivated in Japan for something over three hundred years and are no longer found in the wild. But then the hybrid evergreeen azalea is a thoroughly artificial product and its family trees can no longer be explained only in terms of original stocks that are natural species still to be found in the wild.

An important contribution to the modern evergreen azalea has, for example, been made by the Kurume group of azaleas, and these have been manipulated by the horticultural wizards of Japan for so long that it is quite unclear what the natural source of the plants' stock was. Some experts think that the Kurumes originated not from hybridization but from selection among variant forms of the wild *R. kiusianum*. Others argue that there is so much diversity among the Kurumes that it is unlikely that the whole group could have arisen from one species only and so there must have been hybridization at the start. Proponents of this school of thought suggest that three species – *R. kiusianum*, *R. kaempferi*, and *R. obtusum* – may have been involved in the development of the Kurumes. These species grow wild together on Kyushu, the southernmost of Japan's main islands, and the first two tend to breed natural, accidental hybrids wherever their ranges of distribution meet.

I shall return to discuss the Kurumes later in this story, but meanwhile let us look at the emergence of evergreen azaleas on to the international horticultural scene.

In the 17th century, European trade with the Far East was mainly carried on by the English and Dutch. It was the time of the sharpest rivalry between England and Holland as naval and maritime powers, with the English East India Company and the Dutch East India Company vying for trade throughout the Far East, including Japan. However, in 1639, the Japanese officially broke off trade relations with all foreigners except the Chinese and the Dutch. This self-imposed seclusion made Japan seem all the more fascinating to Europe, and its return to contact with the West during the 1850s was celebrated by an interest in the visual arts of Japan that was displayed by, for example, Aubrey Beardsley in Britain and Henri de Toulouse-Lautrec in France, both of whom were influenced by Japanese prints. A more general curiosity about things Japanese was later exploited by Gilbert and Sullivan in the *Mikado*. Part of this was an admiration for Japanese horticulture, an art form with a strong, characteristic national style. With this went a delight in the amazing plant material from Japan, which could now be brought quickly and reliably to Europe. As a result, azaleas became fashionable and were in considerable demand.

These were not, of course, the first azaleas to have found their way to Europe. Japan, during its period of isolation, had retained links with China and Japanese azaleas began to appear in China during this period – perhaps taken there by Buddhist monks, who were allowed in and out of Japan when others were not. The new plants were prized for their rarity and beauty and were cultivated lovingly by Chinese connoisseurs. Visiting Europeans saw them and coveted them. So, in due course a limited number began to find their way westwards. By the time they reached Europe, though, their origin and identity had been lost or confused – all that was known was that they were natives of Japan. We still cannot name with any degree of certainty the sources of the plant stock reaching Europe, although it seems that many forms of *R. indicum* and *R. mucronatum* must have been included.

These plants were received in the West with great excitement during the 17th and 18th centuries. They were by no means hardy in an European winter, but as tender evergreens they fitted in very well with the vogue for building orangeries in the grounds of great houses – this new and exotic flowering plant made a prestigious addition to the orangery's contents.

As usual, the interest in something expensive and rare produced a spirit of rivalry in the breeding of the plants and the attempt soon began to develop specimens of ever-greater excellence. Older forms were improved in their blooming, form, and hardiness and, since no great amount of scientific method was employed in the process, the steps of whatever hybridization was done went unrecorded. All we can conclude about it now is that the evergreen azaleas, which were in Europe at this time and have contributed to later developments, were of Japanese specific origin. Only in the case where we find a close correspondence with a specimen growing wild in Japan can we make a more precise statement.

Some of the azaleas arriving in Europe came in the form of seeds, and the seeds of a plant may differ as much from the individuals that produced them as human children differ from their parents. Not until modern methodical hybridization was established can we find clear and reliable information about the recipe for making each new plant product. Classification is a human attempt to make sense of the apparent chaos found in nature and inevitably the process continually runs into all sorts of logical anomalies. Perhaps it is by one of these anomalies that the evergreen and deciduous azaleas were lumped together under the one name, but this broad use of the term azalea was firmly established by the time of Linnaeus, whose brave attempt to sort out the complex genus of rhododendrons has had to undergo a certain amount of revision from time to time. For horticultural purposes the one term 'azalea' remains with us.

The Belgian growers of Ghent were perhaps more aware of the oddities of classification than most, because they also produced, to join their hardy deciduous hybrids, the series of evergreen hybrids based on *R. indicum* that are still known to us as the Belgian Indica hybrid azaleas. These are quite the reverse of hardy and many cannot withstand any frost. Their leaves are large, and their huge, brilliant, and often double flowers range in colour from salmon and magenta pinks to a rich violet-purple. In the Ghents the flower colours range from yellow to flame-red. Both groups have white forms. More significant than colouring, though, is the tendency of both programmes of hybridization to produce fussy complete flower forms, double or hose in hose, to gratify the same 19th-century taste for an ornate kind of beauty, which is expressed in, for instance, the style of ladies' clothing or the furnishing fabrics of the same period.

In Europe generally, these Belgian Indicas are treated as indoor plants and they are usually forced into flower out of season. They could be said to have influenced our idea of 'living decoration' for our homes, especially at Christmas. Undoubtedly the development of plants of this sort encouraged the prosperous middle classes of the Victorian period to treat the conservatory as an all-season garden showpiece equivalent in suburban ostentation to the possession of limitless acres. However, when these Indicas reached the southern United States, they were well enough suited to the climate to be quite reliable outdoors. From this fortunate fact, a race of Southern Indica hybrids sprang up in the Carolinas in the latter half of the 19th century, and these remained the only evergreen azaleas grown outdoors in the United States until the importation of the Kurumes direct from Japan to California in 1915.

Europe, in the latter part of the 19th century, was successfully developing its own more hardy evergreen azaleas. In England, some azaleas derived from *R. obtusum amoenum* proved hardy enough for the southern counties. In Holland, Blaauw, from Boskoop, developed the hybrid 'Blaauw's Pink', which is still very popular today. With its salmon-rose colour and hose-in-hose form, this is thought to be a Kurume hybrid (see page 78).

16

From this point, the Kurumes become a key factor in the story of azalea development in the West. During World War I, in the neutral country of Holland, F. M. Koster worked on a number of Kurume azaleas, especially 'Hinodegiri' from Japan, which had been imported around the year 1910. Among the red-flowering 'Hinodegiri' plants was an unknown purple which Koster named 'Malvatica'. This accidental hybrid he then crossed with hardy Kaempferi azaleas to produce the series of hardy Malvatica hybrids. These found such immediate popularity when some were sent to the eastern United States that in 1921 Koster left Holland and set up in Bridgetown, New Jersey. Many of the unnamed seedlings he had produced before the move were sold to C. B. van Nes and Sons at Boskoop, who bred many splendid plants from this stock. So, too, did the Vuyk nursery, who gave us 'Vuyk's Rosy Red' and 'Vuyk's Scarlet' (see pages 38 and 46 respectively). The breeding programmes begun by Art Vuyk after Koster's departure from Boskoop made use of *R. phoeniceum*, *R. mucronatum*, and *R. kaempferi* and aimed at extending the colour range of evergreen azaleas to orange and on towards the yellow that has still not been achieved.

These developments were paralleled at about the same time in Japan. There, in the latter part of the 19th century, Motozo Sakamoto raised seedlings from azaleas growing wild on the slopes of Mount Kirishima. After his death, the collection passed into the hands of another horticulturalist, Kojiro Akoshi of the city of Kurume. Akoshi entered twelve plants from the collection in the Panama Pacific Exposition of 1915, held in California. They were dense, low-growing, and prolifically flowering varieties, already much prized in Japan because of their suitability for bonsai treatment, but they were quite unknown in the West. They created a sensation. Within a couple of years, a Japanese nurseryman operating in California, Toichi Domoto, had established a thriving trade in importing Kurume plants from Japan. Then the great plant collector E. H. Wilson visited Kurume, chose fifty different varieties from Akoshi's stock, and took them back with him to America. The Wilson Fifty, as they became known, extended the geographical range of evergreen azaleas as hardy garden plants, opening up large new areas in the United States and in Europe.

Another, and later, export from Japan were the Satsuki azaleas. These hybrids had been produced by devoted Japanese horticulturalists over a period of centuries, and accordingly their original parentage is quite unclear, but *R. eriocarpum*, the Gumpo azalea, and *R. indicum* would seem to be important ingredients. The huge size of the flowers and the frequent occurrence of variegated or parti-coloured effects in them are two reasons for the excitement these plants have aroused in recent years. Another is the sheer unpredictability of the outcome of breeding them, which turns the process of working with them into a kind of hybridizer's roulette.

The development of the Satsukis for modern use still continues and their story has not ended yet. Hybridization between them and other azaleas offers enormous possibilities. A name to note in this context is that of Ben Morrison, who was head of the plant production section of the United States Department of Agriculture at Glenn Dale, Maryland. He set up a huge azalea-breeding programme in the mid-1930s in which hundreds of crosses were made and many tens of thousands of seedlings produced. The programme made use of all the parent stocks that were then available. The Satsukis played a considerable part in this, although they were only newly arrived in the nursery at the time. A catalogue of descriptions and genealogies of everything that had been produced was finally published under the title *The Glenn Dale Azaleas*. The plants themselves first became available to the American public around 1940, and were much acclaimed. The Glenn Dale programme had produced evergreen azaleas with large flowers of fine quality which were hardy for the climate of the mid-Atlantic States and which were able to fill the gap between the flowering time of the early Kurumes and that of the late Satsukis.

Ben Morrison retired from his government post in 1956 and settled on a small farm in Mississippi, where he continued breeding with a new series of hybrids called the Back Acre azaleas. These include yet more remarkable colours and colour combinations. Clearly the question of hardiness was no longer significant in his later work – the Gulf climate of his new location enabled him to concentrate on heavy-leafed, late-blooming types of extravagant appearance. Their arrival in Europe, even if only as conservatory specimens, is eagerly awaited.

Many other breeders have produced interesting evergreen azaleas in these middle and later years of the 20th century, but their work is too recent to evaluate finally or to set in any historical perspective. To keep up with all the exciting new developments, it is a question of following the subject in the specialist gardening magazines.

CULTIVATION

Choosing Azaleas from the Garden Centre or Nursery

Evergreen Azaleas During the growing season foliage colour gives a clear indication of plant health. In the evergreens, the leaves should normally be green and glossy. There are some exceptions, however – a few azaleas, such as the lovely, tall, white 'Palestrina' (see page 55), have green but quite dull foliage. If you buy plants after the autumn colours have begun to appear, then some shades of red, gold, and orange are to be expected. But always avoid any plants that look pale and drab and whose leaves are turning to yellow – a condition known as chlorosis.

A healthy plant to start with will give many years of pleasure when it is planted in your garden. So look for a well-shaped young bush with three or four good strong breaks coming from the base. Avoid anything that is lanky and drawn. You will probably be buying the plant in a pot so it may be difficult to look at the roots, but in a healthy specimen these should be a mass of fine white threads forming a round, thick rootball.

Deciduous Azaleas Once again the foliage is all important. Through late spring and summer look for a plant with good green leaves, perhaps tinged with some shades of red and bronze. By the end of the year, of course, deciduous azaleas will have lost all their leaves and will seem no more than a bunch of twigs; then all you can do is look for a plant with four or five good branches coming from the base. If, as is probable, you are buying a plant that is at least three years old, look carefully at the flower buds (as distinct from the rather smaller growth buds). Good fat buds will produce a fine show of colour in the following spring.

Planting Out

Preparing the Ground This is such an important task that it can make the difference between success and failure in the years ahead. Azaleas will live for many years, therefore everything should be done at this stage to give them the best chance of success. First of all, think about the planting position. Make sure that you avoid any frost pockets caused by freezing cold air flowing downhill. Spring frost combined with the rays of early morning sun can change what was a lovely azalea in full flower into a sad-looking bush covered in brown flowers. Also try to avoid anywhere in the garden that is too exposed to the wind; we can experience in early spring some really biting winds, which can do much damage to the delicate flowers.

Having, we hope, found a good site, next we must think about the soil. One thing is absolutely essential. The soil must be acid; lime must not be present. Any attempt to grow azaleas on alkaline soil is certain to end in failure.

If you are not too sure if your soil is acid or alkaline how do you find out? Usually it is possible to look over your neighbour's fence – if rhododendrons or azaleas are growing happily in the next garden then you have no problems. Otherwise, you must determine your soil's acidity by a soil test. There are a number of professional firms that will carry out a soil test for you for quite a modest sum. The alternative is to call in at your local garden centre or shop and buy one of the do-it-yourself soil-testing kits that are on the market. The procedure is simple. You take a very small sample of soil from the area where you plan to plant azaleas and mix this in a test tube with the liquid supplied with the kit. Well-mixed soil will settle to the bottom of the tube, leaving eventually some fairly clear liquid ranging in colour from green to dark red. With the aid of a colour chart you can then read off the pH. This stands for 'potential of hydrogen' and the pH scale is the means used to measure the acid–alkaline balance of a soil. The neutral point on the scale is 7; lower numbers denote more acidity, higher numbers more alkalinity. Azaleas need a slightly acid soil – we are looking for a pH of around 6.

I have known enthusiastic azalea lovers who have the misfortune to garden on alkaline soil to dig polythene-lined holes and fill them with specially imported acid soil. This can work for a few years but, sadly, lime has a habit of creeping through the soil. The special pit may well gradually become alkaline and the plants will begin to look sickly. The only real answer to the problem is to grow azaleas in pots or tubs (see pages 22–3).

One final note of caution. Do not plant in waterlogged soil. Azaleas will thrive on plenty of water, but they take exception to sitting all winter in heavy, airless soil. Over the years I have seen many sad plants obviously suffering in waterlogged soil – their roots are poor, their growth stunted, and their foliage yellow.

Soils vary enormously, from light and sandy, through gravel and rich loam, to heavy clay. But, whatever the type of soil, one thing that will do more than anything else to get your azaleas off to a healthy start and on to a ripe old age is plenty of humus. The simplest way to add this ingredient is to dig in generous quantities of peat in the area in which you plan to plant. The more you can afford, the better. It will pay good dividends. I prefer to use the rather coarse, light-brown moss peat, I find it preferable to the darker and very fine sedge peat. Moss peat has a coarse texture that really opens up the soil, allowing the fine azalea roots to spread easily. Other forms of humus can also prove useful. Well-rotted leafmould is good. So are pine needles – many nurserymen use nothing but pine needles, with various fertilizers, to grow excellent azaleas. If you are lucky enough to live in an area where there is plenty of bracken or fern, cut it green and stack it for a few months and then add it to the soil, or cut it dry in the autumn and dig it straight in.

Planting All azaleas have a mass of fine fibrous roots which, under ideal conditions, form a solid rootball. Perhaps the plants you have purchased are container-grown and still sitting in their pots, or perhaps they have been grown in the open ground and are still wrapped in a square of hessian. Remove the pot or hessian with great care. Hold the plant by its rootball, not by its stem or leaves; otherwise the weight of the soil may damage or tear the roots.

Next dig out a shallow hole big enough to take the roots of your azalea, and to the soil that has come out of the hole add an extra handful or two of peat. Plant the azalea making absolutely sure that the rootball is about 1in (2.5cm) below the soil surface. All azaleas have shallow root systems and dislike being planted too deeply. Add the required amount of soil–peat mix to fill the hole, plus a small quantity around the stems to ensure that the surface is level. Firm in, *lightly*. Be careful not to be too heavy-handed over this operation; azaleas thrive in open, soft soil and resent having compacted soil around their roots.

If you are planting in the autumn I suggest that you add no fertilizer; wait until spring and then give a light top dressing. For spring planting a light dressing of balanced fertilizer can be beneficial. I find that sulphate of ammonia at about 1–2oz to 1 square yard (35–70gm to 1 sq. m) is all the azaleas need to give them a good start.

Mulching

The border in which you grow your azaleas should ideally not be disturbed too often – the delicate roots come very close to the surface of the soil and are easily damaged by a hoe or trowel. If weeds do appear it is best to clear them by hand. By far the best way to prevent severe weed growth is to apply an annual mulch around the base of the plants. A mulch is a layer of suitable humus material spread around the plant to a depth that should vary with the size of the shrub. Apart from keeping down weeds, mulching has a number of other very beneficial effects and will certainly add greatly to the health of the plant.

First, a mulch has an insulating effect that damps down too great variations in soil temperature. During the summer months, when azaleas resent having hot, baked soil on top of their roots, a layer of mulch acts as a cooling blanket and keeps the soil temperature down. In winter a mulch has an opposite effect – it keeps the soil beneath slightly warmer, thus protecting the roots from the

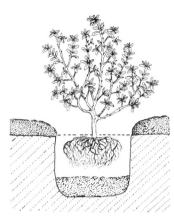

To plant, take out a shallow hole and incorporate some peat into the soil. Make sure the rootball is no more than 1in (2.5cm) below the soil surface.

After planting, heel in lightly.

extreme cold. Another great benefit from mulching is that it preserves moisture in the soil during dry weather and allows rain to percolate easily to the roots below. Another is that the mulch gradually decomposes into well-rotted humus, which makes its way into the soil and helps to keep the open soil structure that is essential for healthy azaleas.

Mulching, therefore, is an integral part of routine cultivation.

Various materials can be used as a mulch. Ground bark is currently a very popular material. Pine needles, if available, are excellent. Moss peat is good and so is old fern or bracken from woodlands. Leaves are difficult – some, such as oak, are satisfactory but others, such as maple, tend to end up as a wet soggy mass.

Two materials to avoid are grass cuttings and stable or farm manure. Both contain too much nitrogen, which will encourage soft growth and therefore increase the risk of winter damage.

My favourite time for mulching all azaleas and rhododendrons is in the autumn (this has an added advantage in that many of the materials we have discussed are readily available then). I would suggest that for small plants up to say 18in (45cm) high, 1–2in (2.5–5cm) of mulch will be a satisfactory layer. Applied annually such a mulch will greatly improve the health of your plants.

Pruning

Azaleas do not need regular pruning. Seedling deciduous azaleas should be nipped back in their early stages (see page 29) and young cuttings benefit from the same treatment. This nipping back will create from the very beginning a well-branched, bushy plant that will need no pruning in later life.

There are times, though, when an old azalea becomes too tall and leggy and then drastic pruning can improve it. A really overgrown deciduous azalea should be cut hard down to 8–10in (20–25cm) from the ground. The job should be done in late winter to early spring. It is impossible to give instructions as to where to make the cuts – the deciduous azalea stem is covered in small buds, so wherever you cut new shoots will appear. You may lose the flowers for one spring, but the transformation of a straggly plant into a dense, bushy specimen will make the sacrifice worthwhile.

Evergreen azaleas are happy to be pruned quite hard if this is ever necessary, but it rarely is. Some shaping during the early years of growth may be called for, but that is usually all. It a plant gets too big and starts to spread over a path, for example, then prune as required in late spring. I normally prune when the flowers have just finished.

Azaleas in Pots or Tubs

Azaleas, like their cousins the rhododendrons, will not survive if there is too much lime in the soil. Acid or neutral soil is essential for healthy plants. If your

To prune, cut directly above whorl of leaves.

conditions are borderline, then it is possible with plenty of peat or leaf mould to improve the situation and achieve the necessary acid conditions. But on really alkaline soils no azalea will make healthy growth.

But you can still grow azaleas successfully even if you do have alkaline soil, by growing in pots and tubs. It is not difficult, as long as you obey a few basic rules. The most important is to use the right compost, which must, of course, be slightly acid or neutral. Your local garden centre will sell you a specially formulated ericaceous compost that is ideal for azaleas. Or you may be able to pay a visit to an azalea-growing part of the country and find a friendly gardener who will let you have a bag or two of his acid soil.

Once you have the correct compost, then find a suitable pot. For small plants a size between 9in (23cm) and 18in (45cm) is ideal. The container does not need to be very deep because azaleas have quite shallow roots. Make sure that there are plenty of good drainage holes in the bottom and drop in a few old crocks. Next fill to within an inch or two from the top with the special compost – I usually mix in some extra moss peat for good measure. Carefully remove the plant from the pot or hessian wrapper and plant so that the rootball is no more than half an inch below the soil surface – azaleas are surface-rooting plants and hate to be buried too deeply.

One problem always associated with growing plants in a pot or tub is that they dry out very quickly, especially during the spring and summer, so it is essential to give them plenty of water. So water your azaleas freely – but always use rainwater. This is particularly important if you live in chalky country. A good mulch of moss peat or ground bark around the top of your pot will help to preserve moisture and at the same time improve the appearance.

Observe these few simple rules and there is no reason why you should not grow excellent azaleas in pots.

Indica Azaleas

Around Christmas time we start to see the pot-grown Indica azaleas on sale in garden centres and flower shops. These are spectacular flowering plants, but unfortunately few of them are hardy in the garden. They will not survive a winter outside in the colder climates of the north; they need the frost-free conditions of the warm southern countries.

In the nursery, Indica azaleas spend their time under glass, except for a brief spell outside in the summer. In late summer and early autumn they are lifted from their beds of pure peat or pine needles and transported, often in traditional clay pots, to all parts of Europe. In the weeks before Christmas the process of forcing them into flower begins; this is usually carried out in a warm glasshouse where the application of gentle heat and plenty of moisture makes the flower buds swell and open. The Indicas have a unique range of flower colour and shape: there are double reds, scarlets, pinks, and pure whites, plus many combinations of pink and white with gorgeous frilly-edged petals.

In the warmer states of the U.S.A. a new race of azaleas has been developed, and these Southern Indicas have now become the dominant mid-season azaleas in the South. In the warm Mediterranean countries, too, it is quite common to see these lovely azaleas growing quite happily outside. But in the colder North we must be content with having them as indoor pot plants to decorate our homes during the dull winter days.

Looking after azaleas in the house is very different from growing them in the garden. Pot azaleas enjoy a warm atmosphere and plenty of moisture and, in common with all this family, they thrive in an open well-drained compost high in humus. Many are still grown in pine needles, which give good drainage but dry out very fast. You should check on the moisture every day. If your azalea does get dry, put the pot in a bowl of water for an hour or so to soak the compost thoroughly.

Even in a cold climate it is possible to keep your indoor azalea from year to year. After the plant has flowered, keep it in a warm place and continue to give it plenty of water. As the warmer weather approaches help it along with a weak liquid fertilizer. When all danger of frost is past find a cool spot in the garden and sit your azalea in the soil complete with the pot, making sure that during the late spring and summer the plant has plenty of moisture and a liquid feed every ten to fourteen days.

In early autumn, when frost threatens, lift the shrub. Repot it if necessary, using pure moss peat as compost. Move it into a warm room or greenhouse, watering well all the time. Given this care and attention your plant should be in flower again for Christmas. I have seen plants treated in this way growing and flowering for year after year and eventually becoming really large specimens.

Finally, if you do want to try growing your own Indica azaleas they do root quite easily from cuttings.

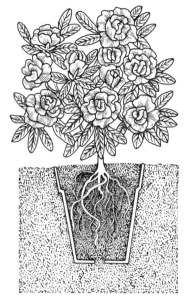

A potted indoor azalea plunged outside for the summer. Make sure the plant is not allowed to become dry.

PROPAGATION

To root a cutting or to grow a new shrub from seed gives us all a great deal of pleasure and a sense of achievement and, with fairly simple equipment and some attention to detail, this is quite possible with many of our popular azaleas. We do, though, have to look at the propagation of evergreen and deciduous azaleas separately. Evergreens are easy to propagate; deciduous azaleas demand a lot more skill.

Cuttings

Evergreen Azaleas The only satisfactory way to produce more of your favourite evergreen azaleas is to use what we describe as vegetative propagation, of which the simplest method is by taking cuttings.

For our purposes, a cutting is a short piece of plant growth varying in length from perhaps 1–2in (2.5–5cm) to 6in (15cm) according to the type of plant we plan to propagate. A cutting can be classified into various stages of growth:

(a) A soft cutting is a young fresh shoot, probably cut from the first spring growth.

(b) Next come semi-ripe cuttings, perhaps the most useful of all. At any time from early summer into the autumn we can expect to find semi-ripe cuttings. Cut a 2in (5cm) shoot from an azalea and bend it almost double; if it does not snap then it is a semi-ripe cutting.

(c) Finally there are hardwood cuttings, which often look like bare sticks totally devoid of leaves. We take them in winter to propagate certain fruits, such as vines and figs and a few common shrubs.

Semi-ripe cuttings are by far the best for propagating evergreen azaleas.

Now we should look at the various steps to take in order to achieve good results and plenty of rooted young plants.

Containers

Use either a plastic tray or a small pot, depending on how many cuttings you wish to put in. Whatever container you choose, make sure that there are plenty of adequate drainage holes in the bottom.

Compost

The wrong sort of compost will certainly bring poor results. The cuttings need an open mixture that will not dry out too fast but which drains well and whose particles are large enough to allow plenty of air to remain in the mixture. It is a mistake to use soil dug from the garden – it will almost certainly contain too high a proportion of clay and silt, so that it will pack down hard, excluding all the air, and become waterlogged. It is equally disastrous to use soft builders' sand.

My favourite rooting medium is a mix of equal parts of moss peat (which is usually bought in compressed bales) and perlite. This gives an open, fluffy mix capable of rooting anything. An equally effective alternative is a 50/50 mix of moss peat and sharp sand – provided that the sand is really coarse and gritty. A third medium that is becoming very popular is a 50/50 mix of moss peat and fine ground bark.

Rooting Conditions

A cutting is a short length of soft plant material without roots. If it is not only to survive but to produce roots then we must observe certain rules.

The most important of these is that the cutting must be kept in a very humid atmosphere to prevent it wilting or drying out. To maintain these conditions a closed atmosphere is necessary. The simplest method of achieving this is to place a polythene bag over the pot and the cutting and to hold it in place with a rubber band. An alternative is to buy one of the many simple propagators that are sold in garden centres and shops – a plastic tray with a clear lid that fits over the top. Obviously, bigger frames should be used if you wish to root large numbers of azaleas.

If you own a small glasshouse it is easy to install a small automatic mist system as an alternative to the closed propagator or polythene bag. The mist ensures that cuttings are covered at all times with a fine film of moisture. This is the most common method used for the commercial production of azaleas. It is very effective, but quite expensive.

To speed up the operation, or to root cuttings during the cold months, bottom heat is often used. Heat is produced by an electric cable buried in the compost. Many of the more sophisticated propagators have this facility, and the necessary controlling thermostat, built in. The system allows us to maintain a steady temperature of 60°–70°F (18–20°C) in the rooting medium, which certainly speeds up the whole operation. But for evergreen azaleas rooted during the summer or early autumn the extra heat is not really necessary.

Types of Cuttings

It is essential to take cuttings only from healthy mother plants. If we put diseased or insect-ridden shoots into the warm humid atmosphere of our propagator it is the disease or the insects that will flourish. Choose a cool time in the day and sever the cuttings with a sharp knife, scissors, or secateurs. Ideally find a young shoot

Top: with sharp secateurs, trim off a healthy 2in (5cm) cutting. *Centre*: remove the lower leaves, and, *below*, dip in rooting powder and insert into rooting compost.

about 2in (5cm) long. Azaleas root so easily that it really does not matter what part of the stem you cut.

If there is any delay between collecting the cuttings and inserting them in a propagator, make absolutely sure that they are stored in a cool moist place or sealed in a polythene bag.

Hormones

Rooting hormones are a mixture of chemicals which when applied to a cutting encourage roots to develop. The most widely used amateur products are in powder form and since they are a weak mixture they are generally most suitable for use on soft cuttings. Semi-ripe cuttings need a medium strength of powder and the more difficult hardwoods need a really strong mix. There are also liquid formulations of rooting hormones into which the cuttings are dipped for about five seconds. For our evergreen azaleas, hormones will help but they are not essential.

Preparation

With your pot or tray filled with at least 3in (7.5cm) of compost, prepare the cuttings by carefully removing a few of the bottom leaves. Dip the cuttings in a rooting hormone recommended for semi-ripe cuttings and insert them into the compost with the aid of a dibber or small cane. Space the cuttings about 1in (2.5cm) apart. Water lightly and cover with your bag or propagator cover and place in a lightly shaded position.

Deciduous Azaleas With care it is possible to root deciduous azaleas, but they are not nearly as easy as their evergreen cousins.

Follow the same basic procedure as for the evergreens. Take a 2in (5cm) cutting, remove the bottom leaves carefully, and use the same open, well-drained rooting medium. The main difference is that deciduous azalea cuttings should be taken in the spring – in April or May. The cuttings will be very soft, so use a weak hormone rooting powder and make doubly sure that the cuttings are not allowed to wilt. Rooting is helped by bottom heat, with the compost held at 65°–70°F (18°–20°C). You should then have well-rooted cuttings in about ten weeks.

Aftercare The result of carefully following all these instructions is that you now have a selection of unrooted cuttings living in a warm, humid atmosphere. In other words you have created perfect conditions for fungi to flourish and some fungi – such as *Botrytis cinerea* – can cause havoc in the space of a few days. So inspect the cuttings every few days and remove any unhealthy, dead, or rotting plant material. About once a week spray with a systemic fungicide – there will be a wide choice available from your local garden centre. Above all, keep everything as clean as possible, including any tools and the seed trays themselves. Good hygiene is essential.

Make sure that the rooting compost stays moist at all times. If you allow it to dry out even for one day, the cuttings may well be lost.

After eight to ten weeks you should see fine hairy roots appearing. Once this happens you should start to give the cuttings more air. If you are using a polythene bag over a flower pot, gradually ease it away from the pot or make a few holes in the polythene. Similarly, the lid covering any small propagator should be lifted slightly to allow in more air. When the cuttings are well rooted remove the cover altogether, and allow the cuttings to harden off ready for the next stage in their life.

Seed

A simple but rather slow method of propagating deciduous azaleas is by collecting and sowing seed. But first a word of warning: a very high percentage of the shrubs we grow in our gardens are hybrids. Over the years plant breeders have deliberately crossed two plants, or two species found growing in the wild, with the object of developing the best characteristics of both parents – colour, flower-size, scent, time of flowering, or habit of growth. The seeds of such hybrids will contain the characteristics of both parents. So, if you collect seed from, for example, a red azalea do not be surprised if the resulting seedlings develop a range of colours, including yellow, pink, or orange. The only way you can guarantee a red offspring from seed is to protect one of the blooms of the red parent azalea with a porous bag to prevent cross fertilization by insects. Then, when the flowers are fully out, you may collect pollen-bearing stamens from a similar red azalea, apply this pollen to the stigma of your protected flower, at the same time removing all its own stamens. By this somewhat laborious method you should be able to obtain seed that will produce red flowers from a red bush.

With that reservation in mind, deciduous azaleas can be grown from seed. In late autumn to early winter collect the fat seed pods from the plants. Do not worry that these still look green, they will soon dry in the right atmosphere. Make sure that you collect the pods before too much frost arrives – in really cold weather they split wide open and loose all their seed. Put the seed pods in a strong paper bag or open tray – not in a polythene bag which will sweat and may make the seeds rot. Place the bag or tray in a warm place to allow the pods gradually to dry out and split open. When this happens you will see the fine, flaky, light-brown seeds looking like small bits of tobacco. You may have to break the pods apart by hand to expose all the seed. Then by using a small, fine sieve you can extract the seed from the husk.

The best time to sow this seed is in early spring, in late February or March, so you must store it in a cool dry place until the time is ripe. When the temperature starts to rise and light begins to improve, then it is time to sow. Again, as with cuttings, you can use a pot or seed tray, depending on how many seedlings you want to produce. I like to prepare my own seed-sowing compost, a 50/50 mixture of moss peat and sharp sand (no fertilizer). Make sure that the peat is moist, rather than wet. Peat from a compressed bale can be very dry, so it is a good idea to damp it down a day before you plan to use it. It takes a long time to absorb water.

Fill the tray with your prepared compost and firm down lightly with a flat piece of wood. Sprinkle the seed thinly over the surface of your pot or tray and again press down gently, to ensure that the seed is sitting just in the surface of your compost. There is no need to cover it with more compost.

Cover the pot or tray with a small sheet of glass or polythene and cover this with newspaper to shade the compost from the sun and to prevent rapid drying out. Place the pot or tray in a warm place, ideally a greenhouse. Inspect at regular intervals and make sure that the compost is kept always moist but not wet. The first signs of germination should show in about four weeks, when tiny white roots should appear. At this stage give more air (as you did for your cuttings) and remove the shading. Eventually you should have a fine carpet of tiny azalea seedlings covering your pot or tray.

If you have achieved a pot or tray of well-developed seedlings by late spring or early summer, then you can go on to the next stage. Once the seedlings are large enough to handle, at about $\frac{1}{4}$in (6mm), they can be pricked out. For this we can use the same peat-and-sand compost but with a very small amount of balanced fertilizer added. The alternative is to use one of the proprietary brands of acid ericaceous compost.

Seedling azaleas can be picked out into small $1\frac{1}{2}$in (3.5cm) peat pots or into seed trays. The seedlings will grow quite rapidly at this stage and a little early pruning can be beneficial. Using your finger and thumb, nip out the leading shoot when it is about 2in (5cm) high. If you repeat this two or three times during the growing season you will have the makings of a good bushy azalea. As the plants grow they will benefit from light balanced-fertilizer dressings or liquid feeds. My advice would be to keep these young seedlings in pots or trays for up to two years, by which time they should be about 1ft (30cm) high and ready to face the rigours of the garden. With luck you will start getting flowers by the third growing season.

Layering
Another quite simple way to produce a few of your favourite azaleas is by layering. One great advantage of this technique is a guarantee that you can repeat your favourite colour. It is somewhat slow but should produce a strong flowering plant in three years.

The procedure for layering is as follows:

(a) Find a healthy young low branch, close to the soil – ideally it should be as thick as a large knitting needle or a thin pencil.

(b) In the area where you plan to bury this branch add plenty of moist moss peat and gritty sharp sand.

(c) Obtain three or four hooked pegs 9–12in (23–30cm) long. These can be of wood or any other suitable material that will not rust or rot.

(d) On the underside of the branch, make a light wound with a sharp knife and apply some medium-strength rooting powder.

(e) With the aid of your pegs pin the branch firmly to the ground, burying it at the same time about 2in (5cm) deep. Cover over with the required amount of peat/sand mix to ensure that the branch is well covered.

(f) Using the third peg and some garden twine pull the tip of your azalea up to a vertical position. This creates a bend under the soil. It is here that new roots will be formed as a result of the sap being checked.

Layering is not always successful, but if, in a year or eighteen months, you see that the layer is well rooted, it can be cut from the mother plant with a pair of sharp secateurs and started on its independent life. My experience is that layers benefit from a year in a well-prepared nursery bed before being planted out in your garden. Do be very careful when you first handle these plants as the union between the root and stem is easily broken.

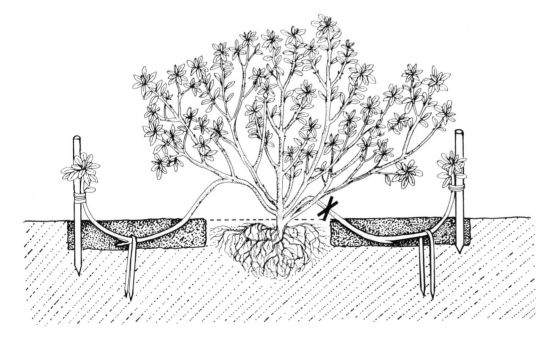

By pegging a suitable side branch into a soil/peat mix and supporting as shown, in about two years this can be severed from the main plant, where indicated on the diagram, to form a new specimen.

THE FUTURE

When we consider the marvellous selection of both evergreen and deciduous azaleas available to us today we might ask whether anything more can be done to improve this range of shrubs. But plants, like many other things, are subject to fashions and we are always looking for something new – new colours, new scents, and new ways to use our plants. There is always something that the plant breeder can improve.

The flower colours of evergreens are at present limited to white, pink, mixed colours, deep pink, and red. So far no one has succeeded in producing a yellow-flowered evergreen. No doubt the quest will continue. The deciduous varieties have plenty of yellows, oranges, whites, pinks, and reds. But there is no deep purple to match that of the evergreen 'Blue Danube' (see page 79). So here again there are colour breaks which the breeders might explore and improve.

Few, if any, of the evergreen azaleas have any definite scent. If we could add this elusive ingredient it would add a further dimension to the evergreen family. Deciduous azaleas have the perfume, but it differs in strength from variety to variety. The common *R. luteum* (*A. pontica*) is the sweetest-scented of all, and if its perfume could be bred into some of the more exotic flowering types we would have a further improvement.

Flowering time offers scope for future azalea breeders. However, since we are at the mercy of the spring weather, earlier-flowering azaleas would be of little value. Instead, we should look to prolonging the flowering season in the late spring and early summer. We have the opportunity to take the season well into June and beyond, and this, I am sure, would prove to be very popular.

Another area that will be explored in some detail – and in fact much work has already been done – is the development of evergreen azaleas for use as ground cover. Because they form dense round clumps they could be ideal for this purpose and when in flower would create a really remarkable picture. For the rest of the year they would form an attractive blanket of glossy green leaves.

The use of azaleas for decorating hanging baskets is already widespread in America. One or two varieties are available there, including 'Pink Cascade', which is a magnificent trailing variety that after three years hangs down as much as four feet. A further selection of hanging plants in a variety of colours would no doubt prove very popular.

There is still plenty of opportunity to find new azaleas suitable for indoor decoration. If scent could also be bred in this would be very exciting. Despite the wide range of plants available now, there is still work to be done, and I have little doubt that enthusiasts will continue to come up with new and exciting plants for the future.

The captions to the colour plates note for each azalea: the height that it can be expected to reach under normally favourable growing conditions; its hardiness; and its flowering season.

Hardiness (H) is defined by two numbers separated by an oblique stroke. The first number gives the hardiness rating according to the British system:

4 – hardy in any part of the British Isles
3 – hardy in the south and west, along the seaboard, and in sheltered inland gardens
2 – requires protection even in the most sheltered gardens
1 – can usually be grown only as a greenhouse plant

The second number, following the oblique stroke, gives the American rating. Under this system North America is divided into a series of zones based upon average annual minimum temperatures. The zones range, in bands running roughly between north and south, between the treeless area in the extreme north of Canada (Zone 1), where temperatures may fall below $-50°C$, to the southernmost tip of Florida (Zone 10), where minimum temperatures may be as high as $40°C$.

The flowering season will, in the United States, also vary according to the zone in which the plant is grown. It will become noticeably later in the colder zones and noticeably earlier in the warmer zones.

BEETHOVEN
Ht 2–3ft (60–90cm)   H4/6
May
One of the Vuyk hybrids,
'Beethoven' forms an open
bush with light-green leaves;
its flowers are a soft lavender-
pink colour.

AZALEAS AT EXBURY

The flower colours of the massed azaleas beyond the lake at Exbury include both hot and cold reds that could easily clash but for the pale pinks and whites with which they are intermingled. The water contributes greatly to the brilliance of this display. So, though less obviously, do the trees, which provide a rich, dark setting for the azaleas' radiance. On a bright day the visitor to the gardens descends through gently dappled shadows and suddenly sees the sun's rays streaming through a break in the tree canopy to illuminate this dazzling scene.

HARDIJZER BEAUTY
Ht 4ft (1.2m)   H4/6   May
This curious hybrid (left) –
derived from a cross between
R. racemosum and an
unknown Kurume azalea – is
an interesting plant. In spring
the whole bush is covered in a
mass of small, deep-pink
flowers.

SOSIANNE
Ht 2ft 6in (75cm)   H1/8
December/January
Every year many of the lovely
Ghent azaleas are grown for
the winter pot-plant trade. All
the Ghents are very tender
and in Britain require
greenhouse protection during
the winter months. 'Sosianne'
(above) has lovely, double,
red flowers, which, with care,
will last for many months.

VUYK'S ROSY RED
Ht 4ft (1.2m)   H4/6   May
A low, spreading azalea with
very large rose-red flowers, up
to about 3in (7.5cm) across.
Raised in the 1950s in the
Vuyk van Nes Nursery in
Holland, it is still a highly
desirable plant (see page 17).

GOLDEN HORN
Ht 6ft 6in (2m)   H4/5
May/June
This is a Knap Hill hybrid.
The flowers are a bright
yellow with a flush of pink
and a pronounced yellow
marking in the throat. The
leaves have an attractive
bronze tint (see page 13).

BEAULIEU
Ht 6ft 6in (2m)   H4/5   Late May
Named after a lovely and historic English village near Exbury Gardens, 'Beaulieu' has deep-pink buds opening to soft-pink flowers with an orange flush on the upper petal.

DIORAMA
Ht 6ft 6in (2m)   H4/5   May/June
A new, very fragrant hybrid of *A. viscosa*, the native swamp honeysuckle of eastern North America, 'Diorama' flowers well into June. The blooms are a rich blood red.

DART
Ht 6ft 6in (2m)   H4/5
May/June
'Dart' (left) is an attractive
deciduous azalea with semi-
double flowers, carmine-rose
in colour, with a marked
yellow blotch in the throat.

COCCINEA SPECIOSA
Ht 5ft (1.5m)   H4/5   June
A wonderful old azalea
(above) that extends the
azalea flowering season well
into June. One of the original
Ghent hybrids, it was
introduced before 1846 and is
still a beautiful shrub for
today's gardens. The flowers
are small but very plentiful, in
colour a brilliant, fiery
orange-red. With leaves
smaller than those of many of
the more modern deciduous
hybrids, 'Coccinea Speciosa'
forms an attractive, dense,
tiered bush. Sadly, though, it
is not easy to find in a local
garden centre or nursery (see
page 12).

ORANGE BEAUTY
Ht 4ft (1.2m)   H4/6   May
A very popular – and
appropriately named –
hybrid. The lovely salmon-
orange flowers give a glorious
splash of colour in the spring.
The leaves are unusually
large for an azalea, with
distinctive hairs covering the
surface. During the autumn
many of the leaves, before
they fall, are tinted with
delicate shades of red.

GRETCHEN
Ht 5ft (1.5m)   H4/6
May/June
'Gretchen', an open-growing
evergreen azalea, has deep
rose-mauve flowers. This is
not perhaps the most popular
of all azalea colours, but it
can form a pleasing contrast
when planted among white-
flowered varieties.

DEBUTANTE
Ht 6ft 6in (2m)   H4/5
May/June
A lovely azalea which carries pale carmine-pink flowers with a clearly marked orange patch.

CARAT
Ht 6ft 6in (2m)   H4/5
May/June
This is an exciting new hybrid which flowers well into June. It is, like 'Diorama', a hybrid of *A. viscosa*, and it has inherited the exquisite honeysuckle fragrance of its parent. The flowers are orange-red and they appear after many azaleas have finished flowering.

VUYK'S SCARLET
Ht 2ft 6in (75cm)   H4/6
May
Another old azalea (above),
but still one of the best of the
large-flowered red evergreen
azaleas. The flowers are a
brilliant scarlet. The bush is
compact, quite dwarf, and
covered in a mass of dark-
green, rather leathery leaves
(see page 17).

HINOMAYO
Ht 3–4ft (90–120cm)   H4/6
May
Legend has it that this (right)
was the first azalea to reach
Europe from the Japanese
Emperor's Garden in Tokyo,
and it is such a pretty plant
that it would be pleasant to
think that the story is true.
The flowers, a lovely, delicate
pink, grow on a light, open
bush.

CHRISTOPHER WREN
Ht 4ft (1.2m) H4/5 May/June
Sometimes known as
'Goldball', 'Christopher Wren'
is a vigorous Mollis azalea
that flowers quite late in the
spring. Its yellow flowers are
flushed with orange-pink and
have deep yellow markings in
the throat.

ATALANTA
Ht 2–3ft (60–90cm)   H4/6
May
An open-growing evergreen
azalea whose large, soft-lilac
blooms combine well with
white-flowering varieties. An
old favourite, it was
introduced from Holland in
1920.

FEDORA
Ht 5ft (1.5m)   H4/6   May
This (above) is another old
favourite – one of the
Kaempferi hybrids, it was
introduced in 1923. The
flowers are large and deep
pink, with prominent dark
markings in the throat. It is a
semi-evergreen that retains
only a few leaves during the
winter.

R. LUTEUM (A. PONTICA)
Ht 8ft (2.4m)   H4/5
May/June
By now almost qualifying as a
native of Britain, *A. pontica*
(below) came from eastern
Europe and the Caucasus
many years ago and is now
naturalized in many parts of
the British Isles. It has the
strongest scent of all the
azaleas. The flowers, which
come in various shades from
pale to dark yellow, are rather
like those of the honeysuckle.
Growth is quite fast, the plant
eventually forming a tall,
twiggy bush. To my eyes, it
has the best autumn colours
of all azaleas – with its
brilliant tones of red and
orange it rivals the Japanese
maple (see page 11).

SUNTE NECTARINE
Ht 6ft 6in (2m)   H4/5
May/June
A great favourite of mine
(right), and aptly named – its
flowers are indeed the colours
of nectarines, deep red outside
and orange inside, giving a
lovely contrast.

BERRYROSE
Ht 6ft 6in (2m)   H4/5
May/June
One of the very best
deciduous azaleas, 'Berryrose'
(left) bears fragrant, pale-pink
flowers marked with an
orange flash in the centre.
The slightly hairy foliage is

also attractive; new shoots
are bronze coloured, older
leaves light mahogany (see
page 13).

R. KAEMPFERI
Ht 3–4ft (90–120cm)   H3/7
May
A fairly tall-growing shrub
(above) that bears large,
single, pink flowers. It needs a
sheltered site because it is not
the hardiest of azaleas (see
page 14).

BALZAC
Ht 6ft 6in (2m)   H4/5   Late
May
The fragrant 'Balzac' has star-
shaped orange-red blooms
and often carries a dozen or
more flowers on each truss.

PALESTRINA
Ht 4ft (1.2m) H4/6 May
This azalea is unlike any other that I know. One of the Vuyk hybrids, its habit is very upright and the leaves are large, soft, and pale, turning to lovely shades of yellow and gold in the autumn. It produces large white flowers with a faint green stripe. A group of 'Palestrina' in full flower is a lovely sight (see page 19).

GALLIPOLI
Ht 6ft 6in (2m) H4/5 May/June
Another lovely Knap Hill azalea, 'Gallipoli' has pink buds which open into very large orange flowers suffused with a rose tinge (see page 13).

CECILE
Ht 6ft 6in (2m)   H4/5
May/June
Deep-pink buds open into
salmon-pink flowers with a
distinctive yellow flash in the
throat. The flower trusses are
large and the autumn colour
impressive (see page 13).

LEO
Ht 4ft (1.2m)   H4/6
May/June
'Leo' (right) is valuable
because it flowers quite late,
extending the azalea season
into June. Another advantage
is that it comes too late to be
damaged by the last spring
frosts. The large, bright-
orange flowers grow on a
fairly open, twiggy bush.

A MATURE AZALEA
BORDER
A fine group of deciduous
azaleas in a charming setting,
against a sheltering wall.
There are no whites among
them, but a wide range of
yellows, oranges, and reds is
attractively displayed. A
seasonal succession is
skilfully used. Above and at
the back of the border are the
dark, shiny leaves of
camellias which have already
bloomed. Then come the
deciduous azaleas. In the
front of the border are
evergreen azaleas, but almost
all of these are late-flowering
kinds.

LOUISE
Ht 5ft (1.5m)   H4/6   May
'Louise' was raised at Exbury
by crossing *R. kaempferi* with
a dark-red Indica azalea. The
result was a plant that
produces a mass of large,
bright red flowers. 'Louise'
forms a compact bush
covered in dark green leaves.

FAWLEY
Ht 6ft 6in (2m)   H4/5
May/June
An Exbury hybrid introduced
in the late 1940s, 'Fawley'
bears white flowers with a
distinct pink flush.

APRICOT
Ht 6ft 6in (2m)   H4/5
May/June
Another Exbury azalea,
'Apricot' has trusses of bright-
orange flowers and pale-
green foliage.

PIA HARDIJZER
Ht 4ft (1.2m)   H4/6   May
This hybrid may perhaps be
called an azaleadendron,
although its parentage is very
different from that of the
original, early
azaleadendrons. It is the
result of a cross between
R. racemosum and an
unknown Kurume azalea. It
is a compact plant with small
green leaves and a mass of
tiny pink flowers rather like
those of its parent
R. racemosum.

SUGARED ALMOND
Ht 6ft 6in (2m)   H4/6
May/June
'Sugared Almond' (above), with its delicate, soft-pink flowers, makes a restful change from some of the more fiery red and orange azaleas. The foliage is a fairly pale green.

SIR WILLIAM LAWRENCE
Ht 5ft (1.5m)   H4/6
May/June
This (right) is a late-flowering azalea, raised at Exbury and named by Lionel de Rothschild. It is a useful evergreen azalea that extends the flowering season into early June. Its flowers are pink with maroon spots.

SNOWFLAKE
Ht 3ft (90cm)   H4/6   May
The original Japanese name,
'Kure-no-yuki', is attractive,
but perhaps the commoner
'Snowflake' is easier to
remember. It is a distinctive
and lovely azalea, with
masses of little, double, white
flowers in the form known as
hose in hose – which means
that it looks as though one
flower is inside the other.

HINO CRIMSON
Ht 3ft (90cm)   H4/6   April
Perhaps one of the most
widely grown and popular of
all the evergreen azaleas,
'Hino Crimson' produces a
lovely show of brilliant
crimson flowers every year. It
is one of the first azaleas to
flower in spring and sadly,
therefore, is liable to be
nipped by late frost, so a
sheltered site is best for it.

KLONDYKE
Ht 6ft 6in (2m)   H4/5
May/June
Lovely peach-coloured buds
open into glowing golden
flowers in tight round trusses
to make 'Klondyke' (right)
one of the best of the yellow
azaleas. The rich tones of its
flowers contrast strikingly
with the bronze of its foliage.

NARCISSIFLORA
Ht 6ft 6in (2m)   H4/5
May/June
A really old favourite, raised
over a century ago in Belgium
but still an outstanding azalea
for the small garden. It has
lovely, double, soft-yellow
flowers, rather more tube-
shaped than those of some of
our modern azaleas. In
autumn the leaves turn true
bronze (see page 12).

PERSIL
Ht 6ft 6in (2m)   H4/5
May/June
'Persil' is named after a
proprietary washing powder.
Its cool white flowers – borne
in big trusses with up to
twenty flowers on each –
make a useful contrast with
the more usual bright
oranges or reds of other
deciduous azaleas.

PURPLE SPLENDOUR
Ht 4ft (1.2m)   H4/6   May
A useful hybrid azalea raised
in Holland at the Vuyk van
Nes Nursery, 'Purple
Splendour' bears very large,
reddish-purple flowers which
completely cover the bush in
spring.

GOLDFINCH
Ht 6ft 6in (2m)   H4/6
May/June
'Goldfinch' has a useful and
attractive compact habit. Its
deep-yellow flowers are
flushed with orange and have
definite orange markings in
the throat.

IRENE KOSTER
Ht 6ft 6in (2m)   H4/5
May/June
A wonderful, fragrant azalea
raised at Koster's Nursery in
Holland. The flowers are
white with a well-defined
crimson flush and a yellow
flame in the throat.

KIRIN

Ht 3ft (90cm)   H3/7   May

'Kirin' is now widely available in Britain as a pot plant forced under glass in early spring and sold when its flowers are looking their best. The flowers are pretty, double, and pink; they are set off by the small, bright-green leaves. 'Kirin' can also be grown as an outdoor azalea, given a sheltered site, but it is rather tender and can suffer in cold weather.

DELICATISSIMA
Ht 6ft 6in (2m)   H4/5
May/June
A lovely old Occidentale
hybrid (left) produced in
Holland by Koster's Nursery
about 1901 and now
unfortunately quite rare,
'Delicatissima' has soft-yellow
buds which open into cream
flowers with a faint tinge of
pink. The flowers are very
fragrant as well as very
beautiful.

JOHN CAIRNS
Ht 3–4ft (90–120cm)   H4/6
May
'John Cairns' (above) is a very
hardy, tall, spreading shrub
which produces a mass of
dark orange-red flowers. It is
not a true evergreen; its
leaves turn a brilliant red in
autumn but fall before winter
comes.

GIBRALTAR
Ht 6ft 6in (2m)   H4/5
May/June
Perhaps the most reliable and
most free flowering of all the
deciduous azaleas, 'Gibraltar'
forms a neat, compact shrub
whose large flowers – deep
orange flashed with red –
have distinctive ruffled edges.

DAVIESII
Ht 5ft (1.5m)   H4/5
May/June
This (right) is one of the best
azaleas for brightening up a
dull corner of the garden,
because its rather hairy
foliage contrasts strikingly
with its pale blossom. The
leaves are grey-green, the
fragrant flowers creamy
white with a distinct yellow
flash in the throat.

AZALEAS IN AN ENGLISH PARK

It is May, and the azaleas at London's Richmond Park are a blaze of colour, a riot of reds and pinks. This is a public park and the paths are arranged to take visitors through the heart of the necessarily large-scale plant groupings. The walks give breath-taking views when the azaleas are in flower, but even when they are not, when there is no flower colour, the massed forms of the evergreen plants by the waterside are always beautiful.

OXYDOL
Ht 6ft 6in (2m)   H4/5
May/June
The large flowers of this Exbury azalea – aptly named after a proprietary washing powder that claimed to wash 'whiter than white' – are white with attractive yellow spotting in the throat.

BLAAUW'S PINK
Ht 3–4ft (90–120cm)   H4/5
April /early May
One of the most attractive of the evergreen azaleas, 'Blaauw's Pink' is a Kurume hybrid from Japan. The lovely salmon-pink flowers are double and hose in hose. It is an upright-growing shrub with good, dark green foliage. I once saw a 'Blaauw's Pink' that made a wonderful indoor pot plant after it had been forced into flower in a cool greenhouse (see page 16).

BLUE DANUBE
Ht 3–4ft (90–120cm)   H4/6
May/June
The name is rather deceptive – the flower colour is closer to deep violet than to blue. I have a lovely specimen in my own garden and always enjoy its display of large flowers. These arrive in late May to early June, and so give a useful extension to the azalea flowering season (see page 31).

MOTHER'S DAY
Ht 4ft (1.2m)   H4/5
May/June
This is an outstandingly lovely azalea that has deservedly won many awards. It is the result of a cross between a Kurume hybrid and a less hardy Indica azalea. Its large leaves always look erect and glossy and, as a bonus, they produce a mixture of red and green shades in the autumn.

SOUVENIR D'EMILE DE
CONINCK
Ht 2ft 6in (75cm)   H1/8
December/January
Another of the lovely, tender,
Ghent azaleas that need
greenhouse protection
against cold winters, this
beautiful variety has lovely
blush-red flowers.

PESTS AND DISEASES

Aphids A succulent young azalea shoot can be quite an attraction to greenfly. I have found that young plants, especially one-year-olds in a glasshouse or frame, are likely to become a target for attack. Being small and green, aphids are easy to overlook as they cluster around the soft new tip. The first signs of trouble from the plant can be a yellowing of the foliage, although by the time this is apparent the infestation is usually serious. Fortunately, aphids are easily dealt with by spraying with a suitable insecticide. I use one of the products based on pyrethrum.

Greenfly normally leave older azaleas alone, but it is worth keeping a close watch as in some years they will attack a wide range of plants in the garden.

Bark Split This is a winter problem, the result of sub-zero temperatures. The cold freezes the azalea and the bark splits away from the tissue underneath. Where the split is not too severe the plant will quite often callus over and make a full recovery. A bad split, though, will not recover. Often the damage is not noticed until later in the year, when you see the odd branch looking pale. The only answer in severe cases is to cut out the badly damaged pieces. The other danger from bark split is that other diseases may enter the tissues. To prevent this, paint the wounds with a suitable dressing. Ideally, to lessen the chance of bark split, your plants should go into the winter in a well-ripened state, so avoid over-watering in late summer and early autumn and, more importantly, do not apply any late fertilizer – it can make the plants too soft.

Caterpillars Caterpillars will occasionally attack azaleas, but they rarely become a serious problem. One insect that may become troublesome in some seasons is the Tortrix moth, which lays eggs in the young azalea shoots. When the active little caterpillars hatch out they spin a web of fine silken hairs around the shoot tip and within this woven cage continue to eat undisturbed. With constant and careful observation it is quite easy to spot these little parcels and, by using a suitable insecticide spray, the problem can be quite easily controlled.

Chlorosis This yellowing of the leaves is not in itself a disease – it is a tell-tale sign that all is not well with the plant. A chlorotic azalea is usually complaining that the soil is not acid or, more commonly, that it is trying to exist in a really nasty soil such as that dug from the foundations of your house when the builders were at work. If an azalea is looking sick with yellowing leaves the best solution is to dig it up and try to find a better site in which to replant it.

Galls In a really wet season this can become quite a problem, especially on evergreen azaleas. Ugly pink or green wart-like growths appear on the azalea leaves and stems and sometimes even flowers. Later in the season these unpleasant growths turn white as they spread their spores. On a small scale your best solution is to pick off the growths and burn them. If the problem becomes severe, spray with Bordeaux mixture.

Lichens This is quite a common problem on all azaleas. It is usually associated with fairly old plants that are growing under far from ideal conditions – probably suffering from bad drainage. Spraying with lime sulphur during the winter months will generally clean up deciduous azaleas. Obviously, though, the same treatment cannot be applied to evergreen varieties – it would destroy the foliage. If the lichen growth is small, scrub the lichen with a nail brush plus soap and water. Badly affected old branches are best cut out altogether.

Healthy and vigorous plants are not in danger from lichens. Apply a mulch if possible, work plenty of humus into the soil, and in spring sprinkle a small quantity of balanced fertilizer around the plants to encourage new growth. If all this fails, you should consider lifting the plants and moving them to a site with better soil and growing conditions.

Petal Blight The flowers may be attacked by petal blight. Small brown spots develop, which, left unchecked, can turn the whole flower into a pulpy brown mass. The problem is usually associated with damp weather or too much overhead watering. If you suspect trouble, use a proprietary spray at frequent intervals.

Azalea Wilt or Root Rot This serious disease can do much damage. Caused by the fungus *Phytophora cinnemoni*, it attacks through the roots and is most likely to be found on young plants. In its early stages the disease is quite difficult to identify. The azalea gradually becomes dull and lifeless, and the foliage turns to a pale olive green. To confirm the presence of the fungus scrape away the bark at ground level. In an infected plant you will find that the tissue beneath is brown and dead with a dark brown streak running up the stem. The symptoms usually become apparent during the summer or early autumn. Sadly, there is no cure. The only recourse is to lift and burn the plants and avoid planting in the same spot for a year or two.

Slugs and Snails These very common pests prefer the succulent leaves of young plants, so keep a careful eye on any seedlings or cuttings that you have in the greenhouse or cold frame. Large lumps taken out of your azalea leaves are usually the first signs that slugs or snails are about, although you may also spot their trails of slime. The mystery is where do these creatures come from? There is seldom any sign of them during the day, as they are nocturnal in their eating habits. At night they appear from under old pots, pieces of stone, bits of wood, or other rubbish. So it is important to keep everything clean and tidy, making sure that all old plant debris is cleared away. Today's slug pellets are also effective.

Vine Weevil The vine weevil looks like a small beetle with a long snout. Only about $\frac{1}{4}$in (6mm) long, it can do damage out of all proportion to its size.

Although weevils prefer rhododendron leaves, they will also attack azaleas. Small round holes along the outside of a leaf are clear signs of weevil damage. Sometimes the cuts are so close together that they give the leaf edges a serrated appearance. If you suspect this problem go out at night and try to catch the weevils at work. Put a tray or sheet of white paper under the bush they are feeding on. Give the bush a good tap and the weevils will fall on to your paper or tray and can be destroyed. If this fails it may be necessary to use a suitable insecticide.

Unfortunately, weevils have a second form of attack that can be even more damaging – and often the damage is done long before we realize that anything is wrong. During the summer adult weevils lay their eggs on or around azaleas. These hatch out and grow into dirty white grubs with a pronounced brown head. During the autumn and winter months the grubs hibernate in the top layers of the soil. Then spring comes and they begin their sinister work. They first attack the fine azalea roots, which they can almost entirely demolish, then they work their way up and eventually eat right round the bark just below soil level. While all this is going on the plant may show no obvious signs of distress, but within a few weeks it will begin to lose its normal bright green colour and look dull, pale, and finally very sick. Sadly, by the time this stage is reached there is nothing you can do. When you dig up the unhappy plant you will find no roots and the tell-tale ring barking of the stem just below the soil surface. If the weevil should become a serious problem, then you can apply various insecticide drenches – Hexyl Plus, for example – that will control the grubs.

USING AZALEAS IN THE GARDEN

Group Planting

The family of azaleas is, as we have often seen, made up of two sets of plants with two very different characters. The evergreens form low, spreading bushes giving spectacular displays of colour each spring and for the rest of the year making useful garden features. The deciduous azaleas offer an equally brilliant display of colour in the spring (with the added bonus of scent) and then give a lovely display of autumn colour. But during the late autumn and winter the bare twigs have little to offer – except in their fat flower buds which promise a good show of colour the following spring. Because of these great differences in growth habit and in impact in the garden, my personal feeling is that deciduous and evergreen azaleas should be kept separate.

With that reservation, it has to be true that azaleas look their best when planted in groups. In the wild around the world rhododendrons and azaleas are often seen growing in natural masses, spreading over whole hillsides or across wide peatlands, perhaps uninterrupted by any other plant at all. In some of the world's most famous rhododendron and azalea gardens we can see art copying nature and enjoy massed plantings of azaleas at their most dramatic. (A list of Gardens to Visit, where you can see exciting plantations of azaleas, is given on page 91.) If we visit these lovely gardens we can learn how azaleas can be massed to give the same exciting effect that we find in the wild.

Few of us possess the spreading acres that these large gardens enjoy – and perhaps it is a relief that we do not have such large areas to maintain. Even so, in our more modest gardens, we are still able to carry out very effective planting on a smaller scale. Separate, quite small, informal blocks of deciduous or evergreen azaleas can make a remarkable impact in the garden.

It is important, though, to take care with such groupings. Azaleas of similar growth pattern should be matched together. There are low, spreading bushes, open shrubs, and tall, upright growers. If all these are planted indiscriminately together the result is an untidy hotchpotch. Colours, too, need to be considered carefully. Evergreen azaleas, with their scarlet, red, mauve, salmon, and pink shades, demand to be treated with caution. I have seen many examples of massed evergreen azaleas planted with little thought given to the association of colours. The result is a horrendous clash of glaring colour.

A bonus from massed plantings is the scent that fills the air from, mainly, the deciduous azaleas. On a warm spring evening the perfume from an azalea plantation is overwhelming and intoxicating.

Siting and Companion Plants

When we consider how to use azaleas, it is very important to give thought to where they will grow to the best advantage in your garden. Unfortunately, many of us do not have the choice between sunny or shaded areas in the garden – we might be all sun or all shady. Azaleas are luckily much more tolerant of heat and full sun than are rhododendrons, but under these conditions their flowers do fade quite quickly. If you have an area of light, dappled shade this will give protection from a late spring frost and the flowers will last much longer and will not fade. On an open exposed site, the flowers may be damaged, the leaves may be burnt by the drying spring winds, and the result may be an unattractive, sad-looking shrub.

Light woodland offers by far the most suitable planting site. It offers the optimum growing conditions in which your plants will look their best. If you lack the ideal position then include a few suitable trees in your planting. The birches are great favourites of mine, they offer the perfect mix of light and dappled shade. All the acers associate well with azaleas. Other trees make excellent companions for azaleas and a more comprehensive list is given on pages 88–9.

Shrubs, herbaceous plants, and bulbs should also be interplanted to give interest. There are, though, some plants that do not, I feel, associate well with azaleas. Roses are unsuitable companions and so are large, untidy shrubs such as buddleias. I would avoid, too, any plants with big, shiny leaves of unusual shape, such as fatsias, and some of the fast-growing shrubs, such as the hebes.

Fortunately there are many shrubs that sit very companionably with azaleas. Always, though, consider how large the shrub will eventually grow, at what time of year it will have interesting foliage or flowers, and what is its habit of growth. We are trying to achieve a planting scheme that remains in scale to our azaleas. At the same time, we wish to include some shrubs that add interest and colour when our azaleas are out of flower.

Many varieties of rhododendron, especially the more compact and dwarf forms, associate very well. Winter berries add colour and interest – try including skimmias, both male and female forms, to give a display of brilliant red berries. Winter flowers are always valuable and for these plant the sweet-scented forms of the evergreen shrub *Sarcococca*, especially the species *S. confusa*. Finally, I would give honourable mention to the range of flat-growing junipers; they blend in well and offer all-year-round interest as well as ground cover. Many other shrubs deserve consideration; a fuller list is given on pages 90–91.

To end our thoughts on various companions for azaleas, there are some exciting herbaceous perennials and bulbs that add great interest and colour. Hostas, with their wide range of leaves in shades of green, grey, or gold, all give colour and interesting foliage shapes through the spring and summer. Hellebores give early spring interest, with their deep maroon, white, and green flowers marked with lovely red spots. The deep blue, pink, or white flowers of the lungworts (*Pulmonaria*) are followed by interesting spotted leaves. The dwarf, spreading dogwood, *Cornus canadensis*, has starry white bracts and also provides ground cover.

Finally, all the spring bulbs mate gloriously with azaleas. Plant dwarf narcissi and daffodils, spring cyclamens, blue scillas, white trilliums, small crocuses, and – one of my favourites – the dog's-tooth violet *Erythronium dens-canis*. To add colour later in the year, use the exciting range of lilies. They can be permanently planted among your azaleas to give groups of brilliant colour during the summer and the early autumn.

Ground-cover Azaleas

One further use for azaleas that I see becoming increasingly important is the use of low-growing azaleas as ground cover. Compact, dense bushes form a thick and attractive blanket over the soil, eliminating much of the tiresome work of weeding. In the United States breeders have raised a strain of ground-hugging azaleas, similar in growth habit to flat ground-cover cotoneasters or low, dense junipers. When more readily available, this new race of azaleas will become increasingly popular, offering the usual display of brilliant flowers every spring with the added benefits of low-growing ground cover.

Pots and Tubs

Perhaps you are not lucky enough to live where the soil is acid. Pots may offer the only means of growing healthy azaleas. The cultural requirements of azaleas growing in any form of container are discussed on pages 22–3. But pots are not simply a way of overcoming a disadvantage. They offer a degree of flexibility that would not be possible for ground-growing plants. For instance, azaleas can be forced into flower early for use as decoration in the house. Later, if you have a conservatory, the first azaleas of spring can be enjoyed a week or two earlier, well protected from the late frost and cold winds. Azaleas are well suited to this method of growing under cool glass.

Another way to use azaleas in pots is to create a fine display on your patio or terrace. Put out as the buds are showing colour, a large tub, or a group of smaller pots, will give you three or four weeks of colour. When the flowers are finished, the plants can be removed for the summer to a cool place in the garden. They will be ready for display again in the following spring.

RECOMMENDED VARIETIES

The azaleas listed here are my personal selection for some specific garden purposes. They are divided into five categories: desirable varieties grouped by the colour of their flowers; hardy varieties; varieties for special flower forms; for special foliage effects; and for fragrance.

Throughout D = deciduous, E = evergreen, T = tall, M = medium height, S = short, and H = hardy. 'Tall' means that the plant will achieve 5ft (1.5m) or more; 'short' means 3ft (90cm) or less.

Favourites by colour

The list is simplified into six colour categories, so that you can follow your own colour schemes in planting groups of azaleas. The information about height and hardiness will help you to avoid planting a tall variety in front of a short one or including a plant of doubtful hardiness in a group on an exposed site. There is no reason in principle why you should not plant deciduous and evergreen azaleas together, but in practice a few evergreens in a mass of deciduous sorts, or a few deciduous varieties in a large group of evergreens, always seem to look unsightly or discordant. You will notice that the yellows are all deciduous and the oranges mostly so, while the bluish varieties are all evergreen and the pinks mostly so.

White

Appleblossom EMH	Favourite ESH
Daviesii DMH	Fedora EMH
Fawley DT	Hardijzer EMH
Irene Koster DT	Hardijzer Beauty EMH
Irohayama ESH	Hatsugiri EM
Oxydol DTH	Hinomayo EMH
Palestrina EMH	Kirin ES
Persil DTH	Lili Marlene ESH
Snowflake (Kure-no-	*R. kaempferi* EM
Yuki) ESH	Sugared Almond DT

Pink

Audrey Wynniatt EM	Red
Beaulieu DTH	Addy Wery EMH
Berryrose DTH	Bengal Fire ETH
Betty EM	Fireball DTH
Blaauw's Pink EMH	Hino Crimson ESH
Cecile DTH	Hinodegiri ESH
Debutante DT	Homebush DTH
	Hotspur Red DTH

John Cairns EMH
Louise EM
Mother's Day EMH
Vuyk's Rosy Red EMH
Vuyk's Scarlet ESH

Orange

Annabella DTH
Apricot DTH
Balzac DTH
Brazil DTH
Coccinea Speciosa DMH
Dr M. Oosthoek DTH
Gallipoli DT
Gibraltar DMH
Leo EMH
Orange Beauty EMH

Sunte Nectarine DT

Yellow

Christopher Wren DM
Delicatissima DM
Golden Horn DTH
Klondyke DT
Lapwing DT
Narcissiflora DT
R. luteum (A. pontica) DTH

Blue

Atalanta ESH
Beethoven ESH
Blue Danube EMH
Purple Splendour EMH

Hardy Azaleas

Reliably hardy varieties are here grouped by height. Noticeably, nearly all the tall varieties are deciduous, while the small sizes tend to be evergreen. An indication of the flower colour is also given.

Tall

Annabella	orange	D
Apricot	orange	D
Balzac	orange	D
Beaulieu	pink	D
Bengal Fire	red	E
Berryrose	pink	D
Brazil	orange	D
Cecile	pink	D
Dr M. Oosthoek	orange	D
Fireball	red	D
Golden Horn	yellow	D
Homebush	red	D
Hotspur Red	red	D
Oxydol	white	D
Persil	white	D
R. luteum (A. pontica)	yellow	D

Medium

Addy Wery	red	E
Appleblossom	white	E
Blaauw's Pink	pink	E
Blue Danube	violet	E
Fedora	pink	E
Hardijzer Beauty	pink	E
Hinomayo	pink	E
John Cairns	red	E
Leo	orange	E
Mother's Day	red	E
Orange Beauty	orange	E
Palestrina	white	E
Purple Splendour	purple	E
Vuyk's Rosy Red	red	E

Short

Atalanta lilac E
Beethoven lavender   E
Favourite pink   E
Hatsugiri pink   E
Hino Crimson red   E

Hinodegiri red   E
Irohayama white   E
Lili Marlene pink   E
Snowflake white   E
Vuyk's Scarlet red   E

Special Flower Forms

Blaauw's Pink hose in hose
Kirin double
Lili Marlene semi-double

Mother's Day semi-double
Snowflake hose in hose

Special foliage effects

These azaleas, divided here into evergreen and deciduous
varieties, are noteworthy for the beauty or unusual quality of
their foliage – in shape, size, form, or colour their leaves are
distinctive.

Deciduous

Berryrose bronze-coloured
new shoots, older leaves
mahogany brown
Cecile excellent autumn
colour
Daviesii hairy, grey-green
leaves
Golden Horn leaves
attractively bronze-tinted
Klondyke bronze-coloured
leaves

Narcissiflora leaves well-
bronzed in autumn
R. luteum (*A. pontica*) rich
orange and red autumn
colour
Sugared Almond pale green
leaves

Evergreen

Appleblossom pale green
leaves
Blaauw's Pink dark green
leaves
Favourite dark green leaves
(hidden by a profusion of
blooms during flowering
time)
Hardijzer small green leaves
Irohayama small, pale green
leaves
John Cairns not truly
evergreen, its leaves fall
after a brilliant autumn
display of reds
Kirin small, bright green
leaves

Louise dark green leaves
Mother's Day large, erect,
glossy leaves which give a
mix of reds and greens in
autumn
Orange Beauty unusually
large and hairy leaves,
many of which turn red in
autumn and fall in winter
Palestrina large, soft, pale
leaves which turn to yellow
and gold in autumn
Vuyk's Scarlet dark green
leaves

Azaleas for Fragrance

Fragrance is very much a matter of personal taste, and
individual responses to scent vary, but these are the scented
azaleas that appeal particularly to me. All are deciduous.

Balzac
Berryrose
Daviesii

Delicatissima
Irene Koster
R. luteum (*A. pontica*)

COMPANION PLANTS FOR AZALEAS

Some general advice was given on pages 85–6 about plants
that combine well with azaleas in the garden. Here I give a
more detailed list of specific plants that are worth considering. I
have divided my recommendations into three categories –
trees, conifers, and shrubs. This is, of course, a classification
based purely upon practical convenience.

Trees

Acer Many of the acers are suitable. Among my favourites are:
A. griseum, a paper-bark maple with outstanding autumn

colour; *A. grosseri hersii*, one of the snake-bark maples;
A. japonicum 'Vitifolium', whose vine-shaped leaves give
wonderful golden-yellow shades in autumn; *A. negundo*, in the
varieties 'Variegatum' and, especially, 'Flamingo', which
produces shrimp-pink young shoots; *A. palmatum*, the Japanese
maple, particularly 'Atropurpureum', 'Chitoseyama', 'Senkaki'
(which has red bark and lovely autumn colour), and the cut-
leaf maples – 'Dissectum' with light green leaves and
'Dissectum Atropurpureum' with bronze foliage;
A. pensylvanicum, for its superb striped bark; *A. platanoides*, as a

background tree – but only if you have plenty of space; and
A. pseudoplatanus 'Brilliantissimum', a sycamore with lovely
pinkish-gold foliage in spring.
Amelanchier The snowy mespilus, or June berry, is probably
best as *A. laevis*, which has smooth coppery-pink young leaves
and is splendidly coloured in autumn.
Arbutus Of the strawberry trees I like best *A. unedo* 'Rubra',
which bears pink flowers. It should be planted, though, in the
background – it grows quite big.
Betula All the birches, with their light, delicate foliage, give
gentle shade to azaleas. Their one disadvantage is that they
have wide-spreading surface roots that take up a lot of
moisture. *B. jacquemontii*, the Himalayan birch, has beautiful
white, peeling bark. *B. nigra*, the river birch, is good and so is
B. papyrifera, the paper birch, but do not dismiss our common
silver birch, *B. pendula*, or its variety 'Dalecarlica', the Swedish
birch.
Cornus I would recommend particularly the North American
flowering dogwood, *C. florida*, in the form 'Apple Blossom'
(which has pink flower bracts) or 'Cherokee Chief' (deep rose
bracts). Good too are *C. controversa* 'Variegata', *C. kousa* (a
beautiful plant, especially in its larger form, *C. k. chinensis*), and
C. mas (which flowers early).
Crataegus Where space allows, these ornamental thorns can
be attractive companions to azaleas. The double-flowered
'Paul's Scarlet' is a deservedly popular small tree. I am fond,
too, of the pink 'Rosea' (single) and 'Rosea Pleno-flore'
(double).
Crinodendron *C. hookerianum* (known also as *Tricuspidaria
lanceolata*) is a strikingly attractive small tree with the crimson
urn-shaped flowers that give it its popular name of lantern
tree.
Gleditsia *G. triancanthos* 'Sunburst' has light-gold young foliage
that looks well as a foil for azaleas and it will not grow too
large.
Malus Many of the crab apples grow companionably with
azaleas. Some of my favourites are *M. floribunda* (one of the
earliest to flower), *M. robusta*, *M. tschonoskii*, 'John Downie',
and the purple-leafed 'Royalty'.
Parrotia *P. persica* has lovely autumn colour.
Prunus The flowering cherries can give both early spring
colour and autumn tints. 'Accolade' is an outstanding small
tree; *P. hillierii* 'Spire' is admirable for a narrow corner;
P. kursar gives rich pink flowers in early spring; and *P. serrula*
has a glossy mahogany-coloured bark that provides year-long
interest. *P. subhirtella*, in the forms 'Autumnalis' (white) and
'Autumnalis Rosea' (deep pink), flowers happily in the
autumn. *P. yedoensis*, the Yoshino cherry, is an early-flowering
cherry that carries a profusion of blush-white flowers on its
arching branches. Then there is the whole array of Japanese
cherries to choose from. I think the double pink flowers of

'Kanzan' can be rather overwhelming, and it has a rather
unattractive upright habit of growth, but I am fond of
'Shirofugen' – whose double white flowers have a pink blush –
and of 'Tai Haku', the great white cherry. You may be able to
fit a weeping cherry among your azaleas, but as the branches
often descend to the ground, they take up a good deal of space.
The loveliest is 'Shimidsu Sakura', which has double white
flowers, pink-tipped in the bud. Of the peaches, I like 'Pink
Shell' – an elegant tree with delicate, drooping, pale-pink
flowers – and *P. persica* 'Klara Meyer' – perhaps the best double
peach, with bright pink flowers.
Pyrus The pretty *P. salicifolia* 'Pendula', the weeping silver
pear, takes up a lot of room but, used as a background tree, its
foliage contrasts delightfully with that of azaleas.
Sorbus If space permits, the silver-leafed whitebeam *S. aria*
'Lutescens' should be grown for early spring beauty. In the
smaller garden, the upright branches of *S. aucuparia* 'Fastigiata'
are attractive. Three other rowans give, in various ways,
delightful autumn colour. *S. cashmiriana*, a small tree of open
habit, carries lovely marble-white fruits; *S. discolor* has
excellent autumn foliage; and the yellow-berried 'Joseph Rock'
also gives autumn colour. A more delicate small tree, of
elegant, spreading habit, is *S. vilmorinii*, which produces rose-
red fruits.
Stewartia Two of the best of these lovely, light, open trees are
S. pseudocamellia and *S. p. koreana*. Charming, too, is *S. sinensis*,
which has an attractive flaky bark, fragrant cup-shaped
flowers appearing in July to August, and rich crimson autumn
colour.
Styrax *S. japonica* is perhaps the best of these snowbells; it
produces masses of pure white pendular flowers in continuous
succession in late spring and early summer.

Conifers

Many conifers make excellent companions for azaleas. The
low-growing types are particularly suitable for the front of a
border and, if there is enough space, the taller growing types
make attractive backgrounds.
Chamaecyparis Many forms of *C. lawsoniana*, Lawson cypress,
make splendid backgrounds for azaleas, but care is needed
because they do eventually grow quite tall. I favour the blue-
grey or green forms over the gold – I admire the grey-blue of
'Pembury Blue' and the bright green of 'Green Hedger'. But if
you are looking for golden foliage to brighten the azalea bed,
then try 'Stewartii', which is an elegant, conical plant with
deep golden-yellow leaves, or the pale yellow 'Stardust'.
Among dwarf Lawsons, 'Minima Aurea' is a dense-growing
golden evergreen; 'Pygmaea Argentea', with silver-tipped
leaves, looks well at the front of a border; and 'Ellwood's
Green', 'Ellwood's Gold', and 'Chilworth Silver' all form
compact, neat-looking evergreens. Two other very compact

cypresses are *C. obtusa* 'Nana Gracilis' and 'Nana Aurea'. To give a change of colour the medium-sized grey-green *C. pisifera* 'Boulevard' is outstanding.

Cryptomeria Perhaps the most useful of the Japanese cedars for the azalea grower is *C. japonica* 'Vilmoriniana', which gives reddish-purple foliage colour in winter.

Juniperus Particularly good bedmates for azaleas are to be found among some of the flat-growing, ground-cover junipers, such as *J. communis* 'Repanda' or 'Depressa Aurea'. *J. squamata* 'Blue Star' and the wider-spreading 'Blue Carpet' are both excellent plants with beautiful blue foliage. The compact form of *J. chinensis*, 'Pfitzeriana Aurea', whose golden-yellow leaves turn to yellow-green in autumn, is very attractive.

Picea The spruces need a lot of space but, given that, they make superb background plants. The weeping Brewer's spruce, *P. breweriana*, is perhaps the most beautiful of them all. The much smaller *P. glauca* 'Albertiana Conica' forms a slow-growing, cone-shaped bush that demands less space. The various forms of Colorado spruce, *P. pungens*, can provide interesting winter colour and form – 'Hoopsii' and 'Koster's Blue' both have vivid blue to silver-blue leaves.

Thuja Two attractive golden-leafed plants are *T. occidentalis* 'Rheingold' and the more recently introduced 'Sunkist'. Both are slow-growing brightly coloured bushes which make effective contrasts with azaleas. I like, too, *T. orientalis* – try planting 'Conspicua', a neat, golden, slow-growing conifer, or the lovely bright green and yellow 'Aurea Nana'.

Tsuga I would recommend only one hemlock to the azalea grower – *T. canadensis* 'Pendula', which develops into a low mound of weeping evergreen branches.

Shrubs

Azaleas, both deciduous and evergreen, give us a marvellous display of spring colour. When they are not in flower we can bring interest to the garden with a wide selection of other flowering shrubs.

Abelia This lovely shrub flowers in late summer. Try *A. grandiflora*, which has pink and white flowers, or the form 'Francis Mason', which has golden-yellow foliage. The small, pink-flowered *A. schumanni* is charming.

Andromeda My favourite bog rosemary is the low-growing form 'Compacta', which bears bright pink flowers from May onwards.

Arctostaphylos This is a useful ground-cover shrub related to the rhododendron. *A. uva-ursi*, the red bearberry, has small, pink, bell-shaped flowers.

Berberis There are some 450 species of evergreen and deciduous shrubs in this genus and a great many of them offer spring flowers and autumn colour. Here I have picked out only a few from the many that cheerfully accompany azaleas. *B. thunbergii* 'Atropurpurea Nana' is a dwarf form with attractive purple foliage and the gold-leafed 'Aurea', also a dwarf, is a lovely shrub that grows happily in light shade. 'Roseglow' is another fine small plant, with mottled silver and pink new shoots. For spring blooms, *B. stenophylla*, with soft-yellow flowers, and the deeper yellow *B. darwinii* give a good display. For autumn colour there is the lovely deciduous *B. wilsoniae*, whose leaves turn a brilliant red that blends with the coral-red of the berries.

Ceanothus The Californian lilacs give just two possible companions for azaleas: 'Blue Mound', which forms a dense shrub with a mass of light blue flowers produced in May to June, and the rather more vigorous bright blue creeping *C. thyrsiflorus* 'Repens'.

Ceratostigma For late flowers I suggest the rich blue *C. willmottianum* and the deeper blue *C. griffithii*, both of which can be relied on to splash summer colour on to the garden.

Cornus *C. canadensis*, the creeping dogwood, is a useful low ground-cover plant which carries white flowers in summer and bright red fruits later in the year.

Corylopsis For the azalea border the best of these lovely shrubs is *C. pauciflora*, which gives soft yellow, scented flowers in March.

Enkianthus This group contains some outstanding background shrubs for the azalea border. A mass of drooping, urn-shaped flowers appears in April or May and in autumn the fading leaves produce brilliant colours. I enjoy the form *E. cernuus rubens* with its deep-red, fringed flowers.

Erica In the heaths and heathers we have an enormous selection of low-growing evergreens that can produce foliage and flower throughout the year. Many forms – too numerous to list here – may be planted in combination to give year-long ground cover and extra colour to the azalea bed.

Fothergilla The members of this small group of shrubs are valuable for rich autumn colour. *F. major* produces also conspicuous white flower spikes in the spring.

Gaultheria The checkerberry, *G. procumbens*, forms a creeping blanket of dark green leaves with bright red fruit. Do not be tempted, though, by the pink flower sprays of *G. shallon* – it is rather too vigorous for planting among azaleas.

Hamamelis Most witch hazels produce their blossom in winter and early spring and so add exciting winter colour when used as a background to a bed of azaleas.

Ilex The gold and silver variegated hollies – such as *I. aquifolium* 'Golden Queen' and 'Handsworth New Silver' – add interest throughout the year, but they grow quite big and need much space.

Kalmia *K. latifolia*, commonly called the calico bush, a hardy evergreen shrub with bright pink flower clusters in June, associates amicably with azaleas.

Magnolia Some of the smaller magnolias are useful. All forms of *M. stellata* are excellent for the smallish garden. I also like the new, compact pink-flowered hybrid clones, originating from the United States National Arboretum in Washington, such as 'Jane', 'Judy', and 'Susan'.

Mahonia *M. japonica* is a lovely evergreen shrub with dark green leaves and lemon-yellow, scented flowers arriving late in the autumn.

Pernettya *P. mucronata* is a useful low-growing shrub that bears a mass of small white flowers in spring. The autumn display of pink, white, lavender, or scarlet berries – according to the form you choose – adds glorious colour to the garden. Remember to include a male plant to produce a good crop of berries.

Pieris All pieris are natural companions to azaleas. The brilliant red shoots of 'Forest Flame' and 'Wakehurst' paint colour on to the early spring garden. I would include, too, *P. taiwanensis*, with its sprays of white flowers.

Rhododendron Choose only the low-growing compact forms. The larger-growing hybrids can be too dominant, unless your garden is large enough for them to form a background for azalea plantings.

Sarcococca The 'Christmas' boxes are low-growing evergreen shrubs that produce rather insignificant looking but very sweetly scented flowers in – as the common name recognizes – winter.

Skimmia A useful family of low-growing evergreens that, in common with azaleas, thrive in light shade. The male form 'Rubella' has attractive red buds in the winter opening to pale yellow flowers for spring. For a fine display of red berries plant the female 'Foremanii' or 'Nymans'.

GARDENS TO VISIT

United Kingdom

Achamore Gardens, Isle of Gigha, Argyll
Ardwell House Gardens, Ardwell, Wigtownshire
Bodnant Garden, Tal-y-cafn, Gwynedd
Borde Hill Garden, Haywards Heath, West Sussex
Brodick Castle, Brodick, Isle of Arran, Bute
Burncoose Gardens, Gwennap, Redruth, Cornwall
Castle Kennedy Gardens, Castle Kennedy, Wigtownshire
Coles, Privett, Hampshire
Dawyck Botanic Garden, Stobo, Peeblesshire
Exbury Gardens, near Southampton, Hampshire
The Hirsel (Dundock Wood), Coldstream, Borders
Holker Hall, Holker, Cumbria
Inverewe Gardens, Poolewe, Ross and Cromarty
Isabella Plantation, Richmond Park, Surrey
Kew Gardens, Kew, Greater London
Leonardslee Gardens, Lower Beeding, West Sussex
Minterne House, Minterne Magna, Cerne Abbas, Dorset
Muncaster Castle, Ravenglass, Cumbria
Nymans Gardens, Handcross, West Sussex
Penjerrick, Budock Water, Cornwall
Portmeirion, Porthmadog, Gwynedd
Powis Castle, Welshpool, Powys
Royal Botanic Garden, off Ferry Road, Edinburgh
Sandling Park, Hythe, Kent
Savill Garden, Windsor Great Park, Berkshire

Sheffield Park, Danehill, East Sussex
South Lodge, Lower Beeding, West Sussex
Stourhead, Stourton, Wiltshire
Trewithen Gardens, Probus, Cornwall
Valley Garden, Harrogate, North Yorkshire
Wakehurst Place, Ardingly, West Sussex
Waterhouse Plantations, Bushy Park, Middlesex
Wisley Garden (R.H.S.), Wisley, Surrey

United States

Alabama
Birmingham Botanical Gardens, Lane Park Road, Birmingham
Jasmine Hill Gardens, Jasmine Hill Road, Wetumpka

California
Azalea Reserve, Arcata
Mendocino Coast Botanical Gardens, Fort Bragg
Kruse Rhododendron State Reserve, Plantation
Edgewood Botanic Garden, 436 Edgewood Avenue, Mill Valley
Strybing Arboretum and Botanical Gardens, 9th Avenue, San Francisco
Berkeley Botanical Garden, University of California, Central Drive, Berkeley
Descanso Gardens, La Canada
Huntington Botanical Gardens, Oxford Road, San Marino

Connecticut
Olive W. Lee Memorial Garden, Chichester Road, New Canaan
Connecticut Arboretum at Connecticut College, Williams
    Street, New London

Delaware
Winterthur Gardens, Winterthur

District of Columbia
U.S. National Arboretum, 24th and R Streets N.E., Washington

Florida
Florida Cypress Gardens, Winter Haven

Georgia
Callaway Gardens, Pine Mountain

Illinois
Lincoln Park Conservatory, Stockton Drive, Chicago

Kentucky
Bernheim Forest Arboretum, Clermont

Louisiana
Hodges Gardens, Many
Live Oaks Gardens, Jefferson Island
Jungle Gardens, Avery Island
Zemurray Gardens, O'Hara Court, Baton Rouge

Maine
Asticou Azalea Garden, Northeast Harbor

Maryland
London Town Publik House and Gardens, London Town Road,
    Edgewater
Brookside Gardens, Glenallen, Wheaton

Massachusetts
Botanic Garden of Smith College, West and Elm Streets,
    Northampton
Arnold Arboretum, Arborway, Jamaica Plains, Boston
Garden in the Woods, Hemenway Street, Framingham
Heritage Plantation, Grove and Pine Streets, Sandwich

Michigan
Michigan State University Campus, East Lansing

Minnesota
Minnesota Landscape Arboretum, Arboretum Drive, Chaska

Mississippi
Wister Henry Garden, Belzoni
Gladney Arboretum, Frank Scutz Road, Gloster

New Hampshire
Rhododendron State Park, Fitzwilliam

New Jersey
Skylands Gardens of Ringwood State Park, Skylands Road,
    Ringwood
George Griswold Frelinghuysen Arboretum, East Hanover
    Avenue, Morristown
Trailside Nature and Science Centre, Wachtung Reservation,
    Mountainside

New York
Highland Park, Rochester
The Plantations, Cornell University, Judd Falls Road, Ithaca
George Landis Arboretum, Esperance
Innisfree Garden, Tyrrel Road, Milbrook
New York Botanical Garden, Bronx Park, Bronx
Brooklyn Botanical Garden, Washington Avenue, Brooklyn
Old Westbury Gardens, Old Westbury, Long Island
Planting Field Arboretum, Oyster Bay
Bayard Cutting Arboretum, Montauk Highway, Oakdale

North Carolina
Biltmore House and Gardens, Asheville
Sarah P. Duke Gardens, Duke University, West Campus,
    Durham
Gardens of the University of North Carolina, University of
    North Carolina, Charlotte
Tyron Palace Restoration, George and Polock Streets, New
    Bern
Greenfield Gardens, South 3rd Street, Wilmington
Airlie Azalea Gardens, Wilmington

Ohio
Mount Airy Forest Arboretum, Colerain Avenue, Cincinnati
George P. Crosby Gardens, Elmer Drive, Toledo
Secrest Arboretum, Ohio Agricultural Research and
    Development Center, Wooster
Holden Arboretum, Sperry Road, Mentor
Stan Hywet Hall Foundation, North Portage Path, Akron
Dawes Arboretum, Jacksontown Road, Newark

Oklahoma
Will Rogers Park and Horticultural Garden, N.W. 36th Street,
    Oklahoma City
Honor Heights Park, Muskogee

Oregon
Crystal Springs Rhododendron Garden, Portland
Greer Gardens, Goodpasture Island Road, Eugene
Hendricks Park Rhododendron Garden, Skyline Boulevard,
    Eugene

Pennsylvania
Delaware Valley College, Doylestown, Philadelphia
Swiss Pines, Charlestown Road, Malvern, Philadelphia
Longwood Gardens, Kennett Square, Philadelphia
John J. Tyler Arboretum, Lima, Philadelphia
Arthur Hoyt Scott Foundation, Swarthmore College, Chester
    Road, Swarthmore, Philadelphia
Morris Arboretum, University of Pennsylvania, Chestnut Hill,
    Philadelphia

South Carolina
Clemson University Horticultural Gardens, Clemson
    University, Clemson
Brookgreen Gardens, Murrells Inlet

Cypress Gardens, Oakley
Middleton Place, Charleston

Tennessee
Roan Mountain Rhododendron Garden, State Park, Roan
    Mountain

Texas
Fort Worth Botanic Gardens, Fort Worth
Bayou Bend Gardens, Westcott Street, Houston

Virginia
Bryan Park Azalea Garden, Richmond
Norfolk Botanical Gardens, Airport Road, Norfolk

Washington
Rhododendron Species Foundation, Federal Way
Washington Park Arboretum, University of Washington,
    Seattle

SOCIETIES

Australia
Australian Rhododendron Society, Michael Dixon, P.O. Box
    639, Burnie, Tasmania 7320, Australia.
International Rhododendron Union, Hon. Membership
    Secretary, c/o 67 Strabane Avenue, Box Hill North,
    Australia 3129.

Canada
Rhododendron Society of Canada, Dr H. G. Hedges, 4271
    Lakeshore Road, Burlington, Ontario, Canada.

Denmark
The Danish Chapter of the American Rhododendron Society,
    Ole. Packendahl, Hejrebakken 3, DK 3500 Vaerloese,
    Denmark.

Germany
German Rhododendron Society, Dr L. Heft, Rhododendron-
    Park, 28 Bremen 17, Marcusallee 60, W. Germany.

Great Britain
The Rhododendron and Camellia Group of the RHS, Mrs Betty

Jackson, 2 Essex Court, Temple, London EC4Y 9AP.
The Scottish Chapter of the American Rhododendron Society,
    Edmund A.T. Wright, Arduaine Gardens, Arduaine,
    By Oban, Argyll, Scotland.

Japan
Japanese Rhododendron Society, Teruo Takeuchi, 8–5,
    2–chome Goshozuka, Takatsuk, Kawasaki, Japan.

New Zealand
New Zealand Rhododendron Association, P.O. Box 28,
    Palmerston North, New Zealand.
Dunedin Rhododendron Group, S.J. Grant, 25 Pollack St.,
    Dunedin, New Zealand.

U.S.A.
The American Rhododendron Society, Mrs Fran Egan,
    Executive Secretary, 14635 S.W. Bull Mt. Rd., Tigard,
    OR 97223, USA.
The Rhododendron Species Foundation, P.O. Box 3798A,
    Federal Way, WA 98003, USA.

NURSERIES

Australia

Berna Park Nurseries, 5 Paul Street, Cheltenham, Adelaide
Boulter's Nurseries, Olinda Crescent, Olinda, 3788
Camellia Lodge Nursery, 348 Prince's Highway, Noble Park, Victoria 3171.
Cedar Lodge, Creamery Road, Sulphur Creek, Tasmania 7321
P. & C. Deen & Sons, Monbulk Road, Kallista, 3791
Hilton Nursery, Hilton Road, Ferny Creek, Victoria
Lapoinya Rhododendron Gardens, Lapoinya Road, N.W. Tasmania
Olinda Nurseries, Coonara Road, Olinda, Victoria
Shrublands, 970 Mountain Highway, Boronia, Victoria 3155
Somerset Nursery & Garden Supplies, Bass Highway, N.W. Tasmania
Tanjenong Garden Centre (formerly Boults), Mt. Dandenong, Tourist Road, Olinda, Victoria
Yamina Rare Plants, 24 Moores Road, Monbulk, Victoria 3793

Canada

Woodlands Nurseries, 2151 Camilla Road, Mississauga, Ontario 15A 2K1

Europe

6.D. Bohlje, Klamperesch, 2910 Westerstede, W. Germany
Joh. Bruns, 2902 Bad Zwischenahn, W. Germany
Firma C. Esveld, Baumschulen-Pepinieres, Boskoop, Holland
Hachman, J., Marken-Baumschulen, 2202 Barmstedt in Holstein, Brunnenstr. 68, W. Germany
Hobbie, Dietrich G., Rhododendron Kulturen, 2911 Linswege, uber Westerstede, W. Germany
Jorgensen, Tue, Rijvej 10, DK 2830, Virum, Denmark
Nagle, Walter, Baumschulen, 7518 Bretten, Hotzenbaumofe 4, W. Germany
Seleger, Robert, Baumschule im Grut, 8134 Adliswil, Switzerland
Wieting, Joh., BdB-Markenbaumschulen, Omorikastrake 6, Giebelhorst, 2910 Westerstede 1, W. Germany

United Kingdom

Baronscourt Nurseries and Garden Centre, Abercorn Estates, Newtownstewart, Omagh, Co. Tyrone, N. Ireland BT78 4EZ
A. J. Clark, Leonardslee Gardens Nursery, Woodreeves, Mill Lane, Lower Beeding, Horsham, West Sussex
J. R. Clark, Lockengate, Bugle, St. Austell, Cornwall
C. Fairweather Ltd., High Street, Beaulieu, Hampshire
Glendoick Gardens Ltd., Glencarse, Perth PH2 7NS, Scotland
Hillier & Sons Limited, Winchester, Hampshire
Hydon Nurseries Ltd., Clock Barn Lane, Hydon Heath, Nr. Godalming, Surrey GU8 4AZ
Knap Hill Nursery Ltd., Barrs Lane, Lower Knaphill, Woking, Surrey GU21 2JW
Reuthe Ltd., Crown Point Nursery, Ightham, Nr. Sevenoaks, Kent
Starborough Nursery, Starborough Road, Marsh Green, Edenbridge, Kent

New Zealand

Alouette Nursery, Lauriston, No. 2 RD Ashburton, Canterbury
Blue Mountain Nurseries, Tapanui, West Otago
Boswell, Mrs E. D., 518 Hills Road, Christchurch 5
Campbell, Bruce W., 20A Waireka Street, Ravensbourne, Dunedin
Cross Hills Gardens, R.D. 54, Kimbolton
Jordan's Nursery, 6 Mekaube St, Ashburton
Opoho Nurseries, Mowat Street, Opoho, Dunedin
Riverwood Gardens, Main Road, Little River, Banks Peninsula, Canterbury
Rutland, Heaton, Stonebridge, South Canterbury

U.S.A.

Ace Garden Center, 3820 Pacific Avenue, P.O. Box 306, Forest Grove, OR 97116
Azalea & Rhododendron Test Garden, 10408
Greenacres Drive, Silver Spring MD 20903
Benjamin Rhododendrons, 18402–A North Tapps Highway, Sumner WA 98390
Berryhill Nursery, Rt.4, Box 304, Sherwood, OR 97140
The Bovees, 1737 S.W. Coronado, Portland, OR 97219
T. E. Bowhan Nursery, 27194 Huey Lane, Eugene, OR 97401
Briarwood Gardens, 14 Gully Lane, E. Sandwich, MA 02537
Bull Valley Rhododendron Nursery, Rt.1, Box 134, Aspers, PA 17304
Carlson's Garden, Box 305–AR7, South Salem, NY 10590
V. O. Chambers Nursery, 26874 Ferguson Road, Junction City, OR 97448
County Gardens Nursery, Rt.2, Box 150, Mobile, AL 36609
The Cummins Garden, 22 Robertsville Road, Marlboro, NJ 07746

Dogwood Hills Nursery, Rt.3, Box 181, Franklyn, LA 70438

Eastern Plant Specialities, P.O. Box 40, Colonia, NJ 07067

Ellanhurst Gardens, Rt.3, Box 233-B, Sherwood, OR 97140

Farwell's 13040 Skyling Blvd., (Hwy 35) Woodside, CA 94062

Flora Lan Nursery, Rt.1, Box 357, Forest Grove, OR 97116

Frank James Nursery, 700 Pine Flat Road, Santa Cruz, CA 95060

Garden Valley Nursery, 12960 N.E. 181st, Bothell, WA 98011

The Greenery, 14450 N.E. 16th Place, Bellevue, WA 98007

Greer Gardens, 1280 Goodpasture Island Rd., Eugene, OR 97401

Hager Nurseries Inc., RFD 5, Box 641D, Spotsylvania, VA 22553

Stan & Dody Hall, 1280 Quince Drive, Juntion City, OR 97448

James Harris Nursery, 538 Swanson Dr., Lawrenceville, GA 30245

Harstine Island Nursery, E.3021 Harstine Island North, Shelton, WA 98584

Hillhouse Nursery, Kresson-Gibbsboro Road, Marlton, NJ 08053

Holly Hills Inc., 1216 Hillside Road, Evansville, IND 47711

Horsley Rhododendron Nursery, 7441 Tracyton Blvd., N.W. Bremerton, WA 98310

Lawless Nursery, Rt.3, Box 728, Beaverton, OR 97007

Mowbray Gardens, 3318 Mowbray Lane, Cincinnati, OH 45226

Roslyn Nursery, Dept.A., P.O. Box 69, Roslyn, NY 11576

Sonoma Horticultural Nursery, 3970 Azalea Avenue, Sebastopol, CA 95472

Stubbs Shrubs, 23225 Bosky Dell Lane, West Linn, OR 97068

Susquehanna Valley Hybrid Rhododendrons, Rt.4, Box 173–1, Millboro, DEL 19966

The Sweetbriar, P.O. Box 25, Woodinville, WA 98072

Transplant Nursery, Parkertown Road, Laronia, GA 30553

Trillium Lane Nursery, 18855 Trillium Lane, Fort Bragg, CA 95437

Verde Vista, RD 3, Box 3250, Spring Grove, PA 17362

Westgate Gardens Nursery, 751 Westgate Dr., Eureka, CA 95501

Whitney Gardens, P.O. Box F, Brinnon, WA 98320

Wileywood Nursery, 17414 Bothell Way, S.E. Bothell, WA 98011

INDEX

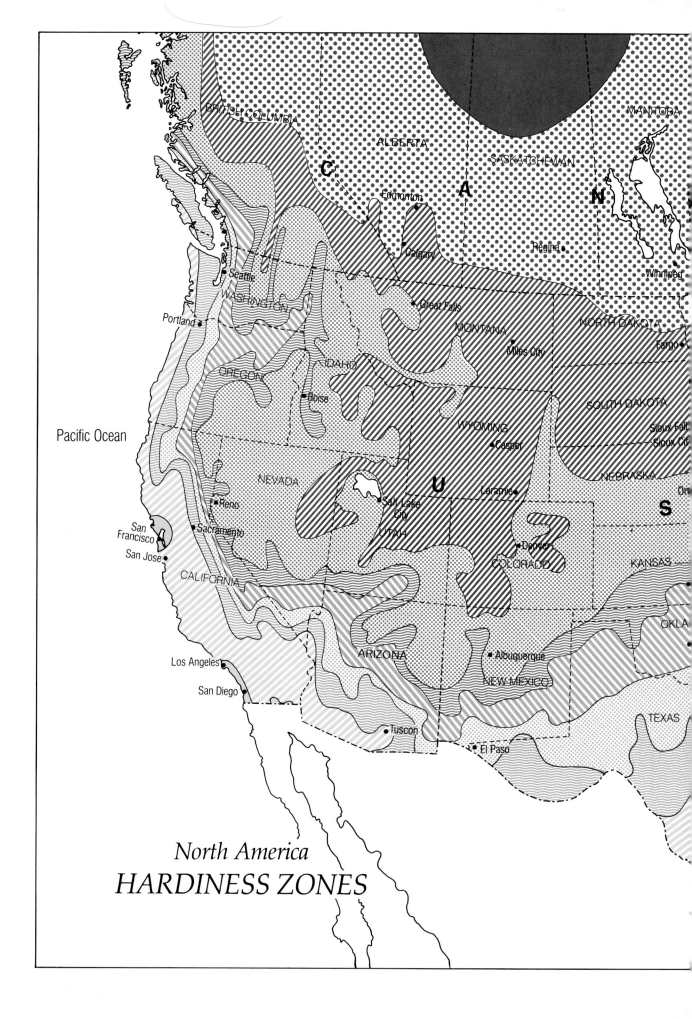

North America
HARDINESS ZONES